theComplete
Graphic Designer

ROCKPORT

BEVERLY MASSACHUSETTS

ROCKPORT PUBLISHERS

the Complete
Graphic Designer

by Ryan Hembree

Design for Communication

The Design Process

Page Layout and Design

Common Design Jobs

Corporate Identity

Branding

A Guide to Understanding Graphics and Visual Communication

First published in the United States of America by
Rockport Publishers, a member of
Quayside Publishing Group
100 Cummings Center
Suite 406-L
Beverly, Massachusetts 01915-6101
Telephone: (978) 282-9590
Fax: (978) 283-2742
www.rockpub.com

Library of Congress Cataloging-in-Publication Data
Hembree, Ryan.
   The complete graphic designer : a guide to understanding graphics and visual
   communication / Ryan Hembree.
            p.   cm.
   Includes bibliographical references.
   ISBN 1-59253-259-4 (hardcover.)
1. Graphic arts. 2. Commercial art. I. Title.
NC997.H44 2006
741.6—dc22   2006008642
                                                          CIP

ISBN-13: 978-1-59253-502-6
ISBN-10: 1-59253-502-X

10 9 8 7 6 5 4 3 2

Design: Indicia Design: Ryan Hembree and Ryan Glendening
Cover Image: Amy Corn, Ryan Hembree

Printed in China

For Gretchen and Charlie.

You each make this whole adventure called "life" worthwhile.

Thank you for your patience, sacrifice, and encouragement these past several months.

Design for Communication 11

Page Layout & Design 63

The Design Process 39

These posters show how fine art
and design sometimes converge.
While they utilize interesting visuals,
textures, and colors, they do not
necessarily communicate a
particular message.
Design: Archrival

Introduction

According to Paul Rand, one of the most influential graphic designers of all time, design "is one of the most perplexing pursuits in which to excel." Nothing could be more true. In this occupation, there are many, unique and exciting challenges that await the practicing professional, including opportunities to work on a variety of projects, helping grow clients' businesses through thought-provoking design that connects with their target audiences, and making a creative impact on how people perceive the world around them. These tasks are not trivial, nor should one take these responsibilities lightly—it takes a dedicated individual to be a successful and contributing member of the graphic design profession.

There are three personality traits that should be inherent in the complete graphic designer: passion, perseverance, and professionalism. Passion is what ignites and fuels the desire to create and it is the reason why we get up in the morning and go to work. In other words, love what you do. To persevere, one must overcome many obstacles and challenges—as designers, we face these tasks day in and day out; not every project designed is going to be of portfolio quality or win accolades from our peers. If, however, we continue to solve the needs of our clients, no matter how mundane they seem, bigger and more glamorous projects will follow. The most important characteristic is professionalism—the ways in which you communicate with and treat clients and in how you react to criticism. Design is a relationship-based business built on trust, respect, ethical conduct, and integrity. Egos are best left at the door; never assume that you are better or more knowledgeable about a subject matter than the client. Instead, it is wise to be humble, no matter how talented a designer you are.

In addition to the attributes above, the complete graphic designer must adapt to the ever-changing needs of business and clients. To help cope with the constant evolution of the industry, today there are literally hundreds of graphic design books on all subjects related to the field—very few subjects have yet to be written about. With this wealth of information and resources available to designers and design educators, it is difficult to gain an overall perspective of graphic design. This book was conceived to provide such an overview and to be used as a resource and educational tool for graphic designers, design educators, and students of design.

Different environments require unique attributes to make them successful and it is the designer's responsibility to think critically about each application. For example, when designing for subway terminals and transportation hubs in large cities, well-lit and easy-to-comprehend directional signage is essential because of the visual chaos that usually surrounds these highly populated areas.
Design: Chermayeff & Geismar Studio

Chapter 1: **Design for**

Communication

Graphic design serves as a method for improving society through effective communication that makes complicated things easier to understand and use. Design persuades and influences public opinion, as is the case with propaganda or political design; design instructs people, as in how to navigate or assemble something; and design identifies and informs the public about a wide range of topics, from a company and its products or services to which country has the largest population. Through intelligent and thought-provoking design, a designer is able to communicate complex ideas in a simple and effective manner.

> " Art [and design] represents a social necessity that no nation can neglect without endangering its intellectual existence."
>
> —John Ruskin

Graphic Design Is Not Art

Graphic design is not the same as fine art. It is true that designers sometimes use the same tools as the painter, sculptor, or photographer in the creation of their work, and they may even include pieces of art within a composition. Both fine art and design are creative endeavors; however, the purpose of each is completely different.

Fine art is typically self-serving, personally motivated, and expressive. The true artist explores social issues, makes a statement, or presents viewers with images of the world around them. Although most artists hope to sell their work to people who connect with their art on an emotional or visual level, the art is usually created for personal reasons rather than for a specific buyer. Graphic design, on the other hand, is a vocation involving the creation of visual communication on behalf of a paying client with very specific needs. In this sense, the designer must address the needs and desires of the client first, which may at times mean making design decisions that do not align with their own. Whereas fine art is purely subjective ("beauty is in the eye of the beholder") and open to personal interpretation, design must be completely objective with clearly defined goals, objectives, and measurable results.

Design identifies companies or organizations, giving them a unique presence. For Theater Brava, bold colors and shapes suggestive of stage lights create immediately recognizable signage on the building and street lamp banners.
Design: Shinnoske, Inc.

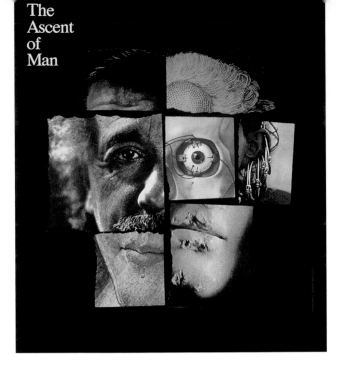

The Ascent of Man

In support of a television series about the history of science, this poster uses iconic illustration, photography and even sculpture to form an image representing human achievement.
Design:
Chermayeff & Geismar Studio

Graphic Design Is Not the Same as Commercial Art

In some educational institutions, and even among clients, the term "commercial artist" is still used to describe the duties and responsibilities of the graphic designer. First used in the early twentieth century, this term is both contradictory and misleading—after all, something that is commercial is produced for mass and profit, while art is primarily meant to satisfy personal curiosity. "Commercial artist" more accurately describes any visual artist whose goal is to sell their work for a living.

While commercial art includes the separate disciplines of photography, illustration, and design, graphic design encompasses all three—the designer uses photography (by selecting or commissioning photography),

creates custom illustrations or diagrams to aide in comprehension of complex messages, and uses formal design elements to construct layouts that merge images with the written word. This synthesis of the various branches of commercial art allows for effective visual solutions that both communicate information and visually intrigue the viewer.

Graphic design is the convergence of illustration, photography, and design. The graphic designer must be the proverbial "jack of all trades" when solving visual problems.

Commercial Art

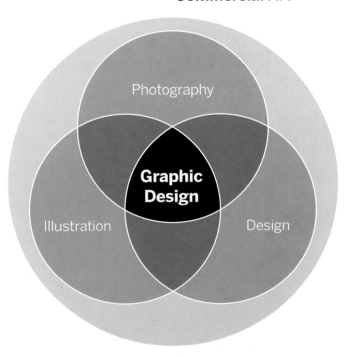

Although sometimes incorrectly considered to be the first known examples of art, cave and rock painting were actually methods used by early civilizations to communicate with one another.

Graphic Design Is Visual Communication

Visual communication combines speech, written language, and imagery into messages that are aesthetically pleasing, connect with the audience on intellectual and emotional levels, and provide them with pertinent information. When properly executed, graphic design identifies, informs, instructs, interprets, and even persuades viewers to do something. It is important that the sender of a message and the receiver speak the same visual language—in this manner, the designer acts as the interpreter and translator of messages. Reducing the amount of information that is visually portrayed creates a more concise and clutter-free design—the goal for all forms of communication.

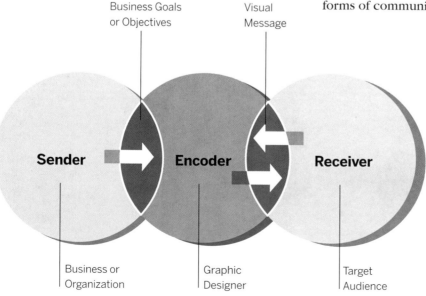

Business Goals or Objectives

Visual Message

Sender

Encoder

Receiver

Business or Organization

Graphic Designer

Target Audience

For effective visual communication to occur there must be a sender of a message, typically a client, and a receiver, such as the target audience. The designer encodes visual messages by translating the needs of the sender into images and content that connect with the receiver.

(REPUBLICAN)					(REFORM)
GEORGE W. BUSH PRESIDENT	3 ➤	●	◄ 4		PAT BUCHANAN PRESIDENT
DICK CHENEY VICE PRESIDENT					EZOLA FOSTER VICE PRESIDENT
(DEMOCRATIC)		●			(SOCIALIST)
AL GORE PRESIDENT	5 ➤	●	◄ 6		DAVID McREYNOLDS PRESIDENT
JOE LIEBERMAN VICE PRESIDENT					MARY CAL HOLLIS VICE PRESIDENT
(LIBERTARIAN)		●			(CONSTITUTION)
HARRY BROWN PRESIDENT	7 ➤	●	◄ 8		HOWARD PHILLIPS PRESIDENT
ARI OLIVIER VICE PRESIDENT					J. CURTIS FRAZIER VICE PRESIDENT
(GREEN)		●			(WORKERS WORLD)
RALPH NADER PRESIDENT	9 ➤	●	◄ 10		MONICA MOOREHEAD PRESIDENT
WINDMA LaDUXE VICE PRESIDENT					GLORIA La RIVA VICE PRESIDENT
(SOCIALIST WORKERS)		●			
JAMES HARRIS PRESIDENT	11 ➤	●			WRITE IN CANDIDATE
MARGARET TROWE VICE PRESIDENT					To vote for a write in candidate, follow the
(NATURAL LAW)		●			directions on the long stub of your ballot card.
JOHN HAGELIN PRESIDENT	13 ➤	●			
NAT GOLDHABER VICE PRESIDENT					

When executed poorly, design can create mass confusion. The infamous "butterfly ballot" designed by the Florida Elections office (instead of a graphic designer) may have inadvertently led people to vote for the wrong candidate. Not only is the layout of the information confusing at first glance, the text is set in all caps and is difficult to read.

Design aids in navigation. For its next-generation global positioning satellite (GPS) products, Garmin's technical engineers consulted with in-house graphic designers to develop a new, easier to use on-screen interface utilizing three-dimensional views of streets and less cluttered screens.
Design: Garmin International

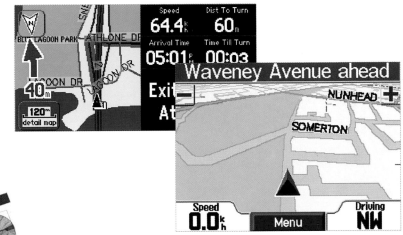

> " To design is to create order and to function according to a plan."
>
> —Sara Little Turnbull,
> Stanford University Graduate School of Business

Design instructs viewers by making complicated processes easy to understand. Illustrative diagrams and detailed photography indicate the steps involved in assembling items, while clear and concise content reinforces the visual message.
Design: Satellite Design

Types of Signs

Icons

Icons are realistic representations of objects or things in the form of simplified illustrations or photographs that communicate quickly. Websites are notorious for the use of icons such as a basket or shopping cart to represent a site's online store.

Symbols

Symbols are arbitrary signs with no apparent resemblance to the object or thing being represented that require the use of a common or shared language or cultural experience to be deciphered. Letters of the English alphabet rearranged into words and sentences are visual symbols for sounds and language.

Indexes

In a book, the index is where readers can look to quickly find more information about a particular subject. In semiotics, an index references the subject matter or object. For example, a highway sign containing an icon of an airplane represents an airport.

16

Semiotics

Semiotics is the study of signs and symbols and their impact on communication and language. Signs and symbols help designers convey unique messages through shared experience and meaning and are one of the most effective tools used in communication. Culture, age, gender, and life experience are factors to take into consideration when choosing visual symbols to communicate a message.

The field of semiotics was first introduced in the 1800s by the American philosopher Charles Sanders Pierce as the result of his work in linguistics. His pioneering work led to the categorization of signs into three basic types: icons, symbols, and indexes.

These are signs for three of the largest religions in the world, representing Christianity, Judaism, and Islam. Additionally, these symbols are indicative of religion in general.

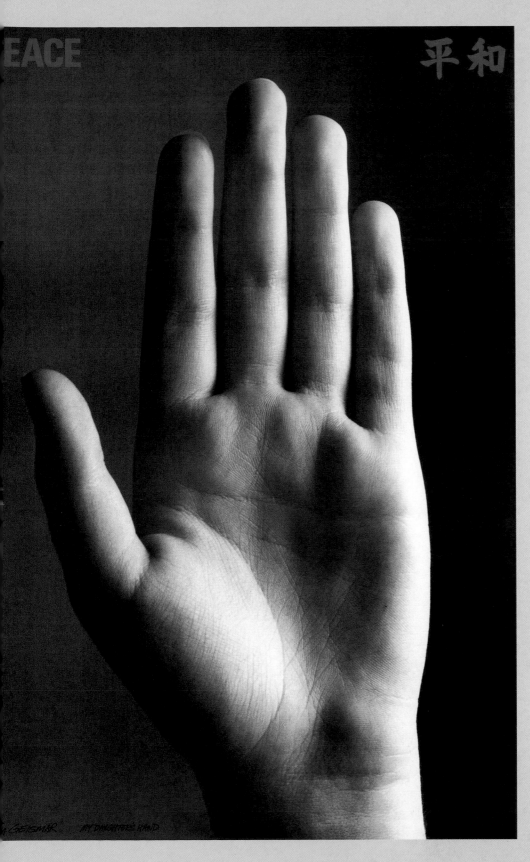

EACE

平和

GEISMAR   MY DAUGHTERS HAND

This poster commemorating the 40th anniversary of the bombing of Hiroshima makes a powerful and clear statement through photography, color, and semiotics. The word "peace" is used in both English and Japanese, while the visual, a hand held up as a universal symbol of "stop," gives context to the word.

Design:
Chermayeff & Geismar Studio

In the ultimate exercise of semiotics, the AIGA (American Institute of Graphic Artists) and the United States Department of Transportation collaborated to create a system of icons for use in airports and transportation hubs that communicate complex messages to international audiences, regardless of language or culture. These timeless examples of design have been in use since 1974.
AIGA/U.S. Department of Transportation

The Meaning of Signs and Symbols Changes Over Time

It is possible for the meaning of symbols to change over time. One of the oldest symbols is the Wheel of Life, otherwise known as the swastika. In Eastern cultures such as India it remains a symbol of life and prosperity and is considered a symbol of good luck. Hitler and the Nazis' misappropriation of the symbol to include acts of evil and hatred has forever altered Westerners' interpretation of its meaning. Because a red cross was used to identify soldiers of the Holy Crusades, the International Red Cross organization is unable to use the symbol in Muslim-dominated or Middle Eastern countries; a red crescent is used instead.

Bright colors and simple graphics serve as a warning to all who operate heavy machinery. Since large equipment such as printing presses are built and shipped throughout the world, visually descriptive icons with minimal text are used to circumvent language barriers.

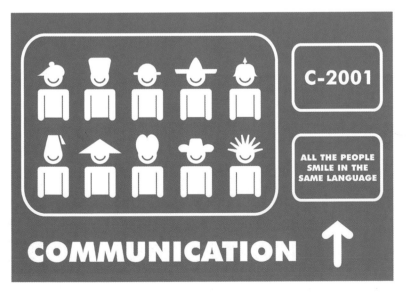

Communication, peace, and unity are the messages conveyed in this poster. Stylizing the ubiquitous "Helvetica man" with a smile and wearing hats indicative of various cultures is a simple yet powerful way to illustrate these themes.
Design: Jovan Rocanov

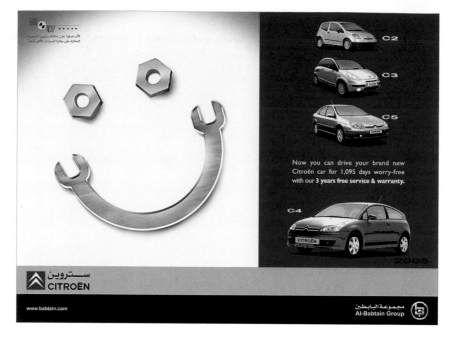

Depth of Meaning

Messages must connect with viewers at many levels beyond mere aesthetics in order to resonate and be remembered by viewers. The more the audience views a message that speaks to them on an emotional level, the more likely they are to comprehend and remember the work. According to Marty Neumeier, there are seven layers of depth of meaning in visual communication:

1. Perception

The aspects of visual solutions that make us look at a piece. Visual hierarchy, contrast, color, and imagery are all formal qualities that grab the viewer's attention and draw him into the work. Multilayered imagery and graphics, as well as other cool-looking visual "eye candy," may pique the viewer's interest but fail to communicate.

2. Sensation

Images with tactile qualities cause viewers to experience gut reactions to the work. Such images have the power to either repulse or arouse the audience's curiosity.

3. Emotion

Appealing to the viewer's emotions rather than his reason has enormous power of persuasion. Positive and negative emotions such as love, trust, confidence, and fear are all employed heavily by advertising to sell products or lifestyles.

By replacing certain letters of a product's name with images of food, the product's intended use is made immediately clear. Additionally, the packaging for this everyday household item stands out among the competition because of its visual interest.
Design: Turner Duckworth

4. Intellect

The power of words in design and subtleties such as wit and humor appeal to both right- and left-brain rationale. Likewise, images requiring audience participation and interaction reward the viewer with deeper comprehension and understanding.

5. Identification

Everyone has a psychological desire to belong to a group, whether it is an organization or a movement. Design that connects on an emotional and intellectual level, such as corporate identity and branding, often forms deep personal connections with an audience.

6. Reverberation

Nostalgic imagery often elicits comfort and dependability in visual messages. Referencing history and tradition tends to resonate with the viewer as being true.

7. Spirituality

This is employed when a work's moral and artistic qualities converge to deliver a message. Everything about the visual communication, from concept to execution, works in unison. Pieces of this magnitude are often timeless examples of graphic design.

Visual communication that connects emotionally and intellectually with the target audience is more compelling and memorable. According to Marty Neumeier, there are seven layers of depth in communication. The more a designer is able to peel back the layers and reveal the core idea, the more effective a solution will be. To effectively communicate with the viewer, different levels of meaning should be embedded into a design, depending on the type of project.

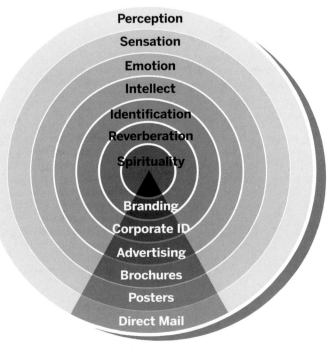

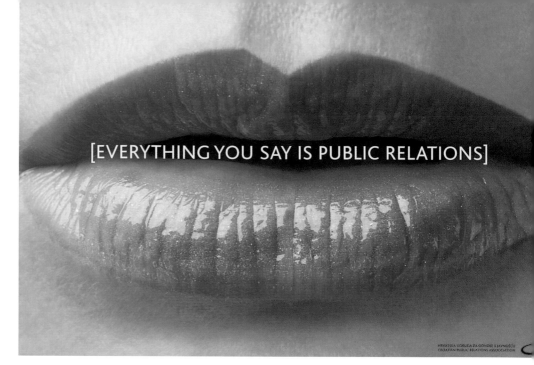

[EVERYTHING YOU SAY IS PUBLIC RELATIONS]

A tightly cropped image of a mouth with a single line of text creates an effective message about the power of words and speech.
Design: Ideo

People are bombarded by thousands of advertising messages every day, so designers must carefully choose their design strategies. Using the perceptive capabilities of the human mind enhances the effectiveness of visual communication. For instance, formal pictorial qualities of images affect the way in which the mind processes information. In western cultures, the use of shading or chiaroscuro creates dimensionality on flat, two-dimensional surfaces, bringing them to our attention. Likewise, rendering objects in varying sizes presents different planes within a composition. This is an oddity in most nations; in many parts of the world spatial qualities are interpreted as flat patterns.

Viewer interaction establishes meaningful connections with the audience, enticing them to participate with the visual message. The audio tones made by telephone keypads are whimsically transformed into a game that drives home the message of seeing "new possibilities." The audience interacts with the work by dialing the numbers to create a musical melody.
Design: Bradley and Montgomery

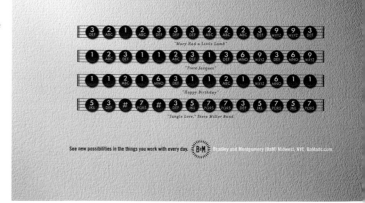

Images that are shocking or sexually provocative often grab a viewer's attention. For this promotional calendar titled "Hot Pink," images of women's pink lingerie dominate each page. Days of the month are placed along a curvilinear path, suggestive of the hourglass shape of a woman.
Design: Ideo

Logos must communicate quickly and simply, and encompass the essence of a company, product, or service. In this manner, they not only identify the organization, they also instill it with values. The logo for InQuizit communicates at different levels—first the viewer sees a red "Q," then an eye. These are not only the company's initials, they also communicate the idea of a person's intelligence quotient, or IQ.
Design: Cahan & Associates

This attention-getting logo makes the viewer take notice because of the inquisitive bunny peeking into a picnic basket. Our minds are hardwired to notice and respond to images of babies, whether human or animal.
Design: Turner Duckworth

This lighthouse uses a candy cane-like stripe to distinguish it from other landmarks or features of the surrounding landscape.

Perceiving Visual Messages

In order to process the ever-increasing amounts of information we receive on a daily basis, the brain collects, categorizes, and comprehends incoming messages subconsciously in the form of visual metaphors. It filters visual stimuli by relevance, calling to attention those items that are most important and require immediate attention.

Human physiology allows for the quick detection of rapid change to serve as a warning of impending danger. A flashing red light at an intersection indicates that motorists should stop. Lighthouses are painted in striped patterns to prevent them from blending into the horizon or surrounding land formations during the day. In nature, venomous creatures such as snakes have angular and geometric patterns to warn others of their danger. Slow and incremental change, on the other hand, is harder for the eye to detect.

The design of this product's packaging connects with consumers in an unexpected way and appeals to the intelligence of shoppers through wit. Instead of showing a photograph of the product in use, this minimalist design features items that are sticky and messy, and would require the use of the product.
Design: Turner Duckworth

Context

Countries in North America and northern Europe are considered "low-context" societies, in which the content of visual messages is interpreted literally. Organization, categorization, and the presentation of information for clarity and comprehension are the most essential qualities of effective communication in these regions. Executive summaries and bullet-point text are preferred to long-winded, descriptive paragraphs, and images requiring little effort to decipher are preferred over visually complex and symbolic ones. Instead of assuming that audiences are intelligent and relatively intuitive, designers tend to create visual solutions that communicate to the least-educated person, often with redundancy of information and design elements or by replacing words with symbols.

High-context societies such as Asia, eastern Europe, and Latin America respond to an aesthetic that utilizes many layers of depth and meaning, in contrast to the instant-gratification mentality of low-context cultures. Shared cultural experiences or educational backgrounds allow visual messages to be understood and comprehended without literal explanation or redundant information. Designers appeal directly to the intellect of their audience through messages that are only relevant to them, much like an "inside joke" or story. They challenge viewers to decipher visually sophisticated imagery or symbolism, which leads to greater satisfaction, emotional connection, and memorability.

Appealing to the viewer's intellect makes a logo more memorable. At first glance, this logo conveys the idea of fire through flames. Upon closer examination, an alternate image of lovers kissing is revealed. This dual visual reinforces the company name and rewards the viewer.
Design: Brainding

This book cover may appeal more to high-context audiences in that the viewer must decipher symbolism and imagery to receive the intended message. Light bulbs are normally cliché when representing "bright ideas," however this book cover takes the concept one step further by covering the bulb in foliage, which is representative of the environment, thus reinforcing the title, *Wisdom for a Livable Planet*.
Design: Pentagram

THE VISIONARY WORK OF TERRI SWEARINGEN, DAVE FOREMAN, WES JACKSON, HELENA NORBERG-HODGE, WERNER FORNOS, HERMAN DALY, STEPHEN SCHNEIDER, AND DAVID ORR

Wisdom *for a* Livable Planet

CARL N. MCDANIEL

High-context audiences require very little written copy to receive a message. In these ad concepts for a restaurant and wine bar, a bottle of wine and simple line illustrations form a bull (suggestive of steak) and fish (suggestive of seafood). The taglines are almost unnecessary because of the strong visual images and color associations.
Design: Jovan Rocanov

con carne

con pescado

These flash cards and annual report use whimsical illustrations to teach children basic words and concepts. Higher-context societies are more likely to regard the front of these cards as being more communicative than the back since they contain far more information spelled out in great detail.
Design: Greteman Group

Cultural Considerations in Communication

Our world is becoming an increasingly smaller place through mass communication and technological achievement. As a result, it is not uncommon for the designer to create a piece that will be viewed by people from different parts of the world. Therefore, understanding and incorporating the cultural experience of one's audience is extremely important when designing for international audiences.

A "culture" is a series of learned preferences depending on one's geographic location, ethnicity, and educational background. People with similar life experiences better relate to one another through a similar vocabulary of imagery, symbols, and clichés. Because effective communication occurs through these shared cultural experiences, learning the subtleties and nuances of each country or culture will greatly enhance the effectiveness of one's design.

The American saying, "laughter is the best medicine," is effectively communicated in this poster for a play called Wit. This message is conveyed to the audience through a whimsical illustration.
Design: Modern Dog

Governments around the world have long been patrons of the arts, commissioning graphic designs for paper currency and even postage stamps. These books of stamps for the Royal Mail use color-coding and large typography to quickly communicate denominations for different types of stamps.
Design: CDT Design

The Communicative Quality of Color

Color has the ability to evoke powerful emotions from people, so when used properly, it can be a highly effective tool for communication. Although cultural associations of color vary, there are some commonalities in terms of color preference and meaning. The three primary colors—red, yellow, and blue—tend to be the colors most people are drawn to. For example, the most popular color in the world among adults, male and female, is blue. Among children, red is the preferred color, while yellow, the most luminous color in the spectrum, tends to draw the attention of infants and toddlers with developing vision.

Red is the most passionate color and tends to excite and get adrenaline pumping through the body. It is associated with both love and anger; it can mean good luck, represent lust or adultery (as in *The Scarlet Letter* or a "red light" district), danger, and also helps to incite warfare (the ancient Romans carried red flags into battle because of the color's association with blood).

Blue, the most popular color, universally symbolizes serenity and tranquility. It has a calming effect if used in moderation or suggests a deep depression if the viewer is inundated with too much blue. Part of this color's soothing quali-

The new Food Pyramid released by the U.S. Food and Drug Administration uses different color wedges to represent the daily recommended portions for various types of foods, a simplified version of the old, higher-context Food Pyramid.

Color Meaning and Association

Brown
- flavorful, suggestive of meat, chocolate, and bread
- associated with earthiness
- richness
- warmth and comfort
- mellowness

Black
- color of mourning in Western cultures
- suggestive of darkness, night, or evil
- elegance, such as "black tie" events

White
- color worn at weddings in Western cultures
- symbolic of purity, cleanliness, or goodness
- color of mourning in Asian cultures

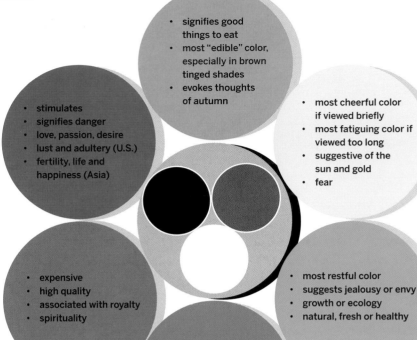

- signifies good things to eat
- most "edible" color, especially in brown tinged shades
- evokes thoughts of autumn

- stimulates
- signifies danger
- love, passion, desire
- lust and adultery (U.S.)
- fertility, life and happiness (Asia)

- most cheerful color if viewed briefly
- most fatiguing color if viewed too long
- suggestive of the sun and gold
- fear

- expensive
- high quality
- associated with royalty
- spirituality

- most restful color
- suggests jealousy or envy
- growth or ecology
- natural, fresh or healthy

- relaxing
- serenity
- suggestive of the sea and sky
- frozen or cold

ties and appeal are attributed to the sky and ocean. Blue is a cool color and is often associated with cold things, such as frozen food. Additionally, blue is suggestive of both quality and expertise (blue ribbons are given to first-place winners). Because of these positive attributes, blue is the most popular and widely specified color in corporate identity programs.

Yellow is the most luminous color of the spectrum. Because of its high visibility, warning signs are often painted this color. Yellow traditionally represents the sun and is a most cheerful color when used in moderation. If used too

Design for Communication

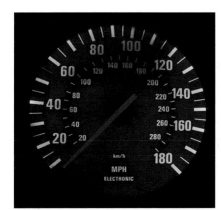

To aid in nighttime driving, most automobile dashboard displays use green-white or blue-white illumination because they are easiest to see. As the eyes age, they tend to yellow, making red-illuminated dashboards, such as those found in sports cars and fighter jets, more difficult to read.

Green is a cool color with soothing properties similar to blue. This relaxing hue is associated with growth and prosperity as well as health and wellness. It can also suggest envy and jealousy, such as the "green-eyed monster" described in Shakespeare's *Othello*.

Orange is a warm color often associated with fire and good things to eat. And so it is the most edible color, which explains why many fast foods chains use it as part of their color scheme.

Purple is universally associated with both royalty and spirituality because in ancient times only emperors or kings could afford garments made of purple dye. The naturally occurring dye for Tyrian purple is extremely rare because it is extracted from small mollusks that inhabit the Mediterranean Sea. It takes 9,000 mollusks to yield one-third ounce (one gram) of purple dye.

Pastel colors are generally considered to be feminine and are used to represent sentiments such as caring and gentleness. Pastels, often used as colors for nurseries, are gender specific: light blue for a boy, and pink for a girl. Additionally, because pink has a calming and sedating effect, it is often used in hospital waiting rooms.

Lance Armstrong, seven-time winner of the Tour de France, created the "Livestrong" brand to help raise awareness of and support cancer research. A cancer survivor himself, Armstrong designed these simple yellow bracelets, to serve as a symbol of strength and a reminder of hope.

liberally, it can tire the eyes and make people irritable (couples with yellow kitchens tend to argue more often when in those areas). Conversely, yellow has also become synonymous with greed and cowardliness (in tenth-century France, the doors of traitors and criminals were painted yellow).

Colors are also often associated with different social or political causes because of the strong emotions associated with them. In the Ukraine, Viktor Yanukovych's party adopted the color orange and their fight to have the vote recast was deemed the "Orange Revolution." In the United States, red and blue are politically charged colors symbolic of moral or ideological beliefs, with blue representing the Democratic Party and red representing the Republican Party (although this has not always been the case—before the 1996 presidential election, the color schemes were reversed and blue was the color of the incumbent party). Yellow ribbons have been used to support the armed forces, while pink and red ribbons have been used to raise awareness of breast cancer and the impact of AIDS.

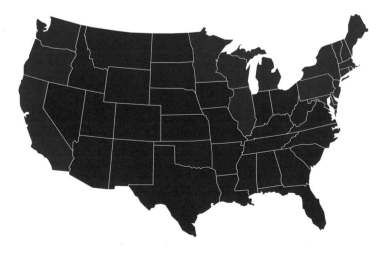

Following the 2004 U.S. Presidential Election, people began to identify "red states" and "blue states," associated with the ideological beliefs of the Republican and Democratic political parties, respectively.

Feminine color palettes, unique illustration styles, and a nontraditional package format make these chocolates stand out from other competing products.
Design: Brainding

Color Implications Across Cultures

Color is a very powerful element of design and represents a unique and often difficult challenge for the designer. Color association differs between cultures and is increasingly necessary for the designer to consider when designing for multicultural audiences. What might be considered appropriate for one country or audience might be considered inappropriate, if not offensive, in another.

White is considered a symbol of purity and goodness in Western culture and is traditionally worn at weddings; in Asia, it represents death and mourning and is worn at funerals (in North America, black is the traditional mourning color). Red is symbolic of lust and adultery in the United States, yet in Asia it is the color worn at weddings as a symbol of good luck and fertility. Being in tune to these types of color preferences allows the designer to be sure that the proper message is being communicated to the target audience.

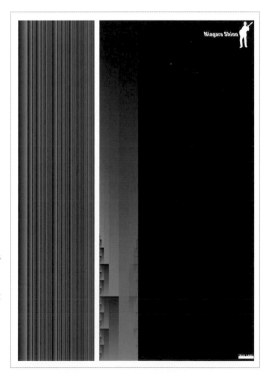

Cool colors such as blue and green have a calming, sedating effect on the viewer. Various shades of blue within this poster, along with the static qualities of vertical lines, make an attractive piece that communicates an almost meditative feeling.
Design: Shinnoske, Inc.

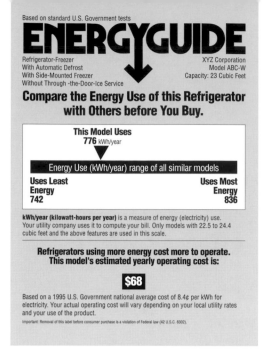

Based on standard U.S. Government tests

ENERGYGUIDE

Refrigerator-Freezer
With Automatic Defrost
With Side-Mounted Freezer
Without Through -the-Door-Ice Service

XYZ Corporation
Model ABC-W
Capacity: 23 Cubic Feet

Compare the Energy Use of this Refrigerator with Others before You Buy.

This Model Uses
776 kWh/year

Energy Use (kWh/year) range of all similar models

**Uses Least
Energy
742**

**Uses Most
Energy
836**

kWh/year (kilowatt-hours per year) is a measure of energy (electricity) use. Your utility company uses it to compute your bill. Only models with 22.5 to 24.4 cubic feet and the above features are used in this scale.

**Refrigerators using more energy cost more to operate.
This model's estimated yearly operating cost is:**

$68

Based on a 1995 U.S. Government national average cost of 8.4¢ per kWh for electricity. Your actual operating cost will vary depending on your local utility rates and your use of the product.

Important: Removal of this label before consumer purchase is a violation of Federal law (42 U.S.C. 6302).

Bright yellow informational stickers are placed on major appliances to educate consumers about their energy usage. They also make it easier to comparison-shop between brands of merchandise.
Design: Burkey Belser, U.S. Federal Trade Commission

The Role of Design in Everyday Life

Governments around the world recognize the importance of controlling and disseminating information. To better facilitate user comprehension, they often regulate various documents and packaging. Official documents such as tax forms and visa applications must be easy to use and comprehend. Nutrition labels as well as product labels and safety guidelines must appear on food packages. In each of these examples of government communication, the standards require that information be presented in a consistent manner on every product so viewers do not have trouble correctly deciphering the content or making informed buying decisions.

The tax codes of most countries are very complex, sometimes requiring thousands of pages of rules and regulations. To ensure that citizens understand their financial obligation to the government, forms are designed in a manner that all citizens can easily understand and use. For the British Tax Council, helpful tip boxes and shaded content areas are employed for ease of use. (After its redesign in 2002, on-time payments increased 80 percent, according to the Design Council.)

Part 2 About you and your partner (If you have one)

Help notes From the 5th December, a partner means a person you are married to or have a civil partnership with, or a person you live with as if you were their husband, wife or civil partner. (A civil partner is a formal arrangement that gives same-sex partners the same legal status as a married couple.)

Proof needed We must see proof of identity and National Insurance number for you and your partner, if you have one. We also need to see proof of your immigration status if you are from abroad. See the checklist on pages 26 and 27 for details of the type of proof we need to see. We must see original documents, not photocopies.

Do you have a partner who normally lives with you? | Answer 'Yes' or 'No' | If 'Yes', you must answer all the questions about them as well.

	You	Your partner
Your title (Mr, Miss, Mrs, Ms)		
Your last name		
Your first names		
Your date of birth		
Your National Insurance number (You will find this on your ES40, pension book, tax letters or wage slips.)		
Any other name you have been known by		

Have you ever claimed Housing Benefit or Council Tax Benefit before?
If 'Yes', when did you last claim? | 'Yes' or 'No' | 'Yes' or 'No'

Which council did you claim from? | |
What name did you use when you claimed? | |
Please give the address you claimed for, if it was different to your current address. | |

Give the date you moved into your current address. | |
Is this an exact date? | 'Yes' or 'No' | 'Yes' or 'No'
If this was in the last 12 months, give your previous address.

> " Information designers are very special people who must master all the skills and talents of a designer, combine it with the rigor and problem solving ability of a scientist or mathematician, and bring the curiosity, research skills, and doggedness of a scholar to their work."
>
> —Terry Irwin

Design for Public Service

As effective communicators, graphic designers have enormous power and responsibility to use their craft for good and noble purposes or for causes they believe in. In times of conflict and revolution, design provides the government with propaganda, urging citizens to take action. During World War II, posters from the Office of War Information encouraged citizens to help the war effort through conservation and increased factory production. The atrocities committed within Nazi concentration camps were also exposed through war-related propaganda and design.

In addition to fulfilling the needs of government propaganda, design has traditionally been essential to promoting causes for the greater human good. Throughout history, designers have banded together to develop communication pieces that raised awareness about social and political issues in an effort to force a positive change. Because these types of projects are often highly conceptual and offer great freedom, many designers find self-initiated and pro bono projects more gratifying than traditional paying commissions.

Nutrition Facts

Serving Size 3/4 cup (30g)
Servings Per Container 11

Amount Per Serving

Calories 100   Calories from Fat 11

	% Daily Value*
Total Fat 1g	**1%**
Saturated Fat 0	**0%**
Trans Fat 3g	
Cholesterol 0mg	**0%**
Sodium 200 mg	**8%**
Total Carbohydrate 24g	**8%**
Dietary Fiber 3g	**10%**
Sugars 5g	
Protein 2g	
Vitamin A	100%
Vitamin C	100%
Calcium	25%
Iron	100%

* Percent Daily Values are based on a 2,000 calorie diet. Your daily values may be higher or lower depending on your calorie needs:

		Calories:	2,000	2,500
Total Fat	Less than		65g	80g
Sat Fat	Less than		20g	25g
Cholesterol	Less than		300mg	375mg
Total Carbohydrate			300g	375g
Dietary Fiber			25g	30g

Communicating nutrition information is a governmentally regulated necessity for all food products sold in the United States and abroad. The nutrition label has undergone many design revisions as the needs and dietary habits of American citizens change.
Design: Burkey Belser

In this series of posters for the United Nations, statistics on inequality are powerfully projected to the viewer through the simple use of type and color. The layout of the supporting typography on the side of each poster is visually reminiscent of a ruler or other measuring device.
Design: Chermayeff & Geismar Studio

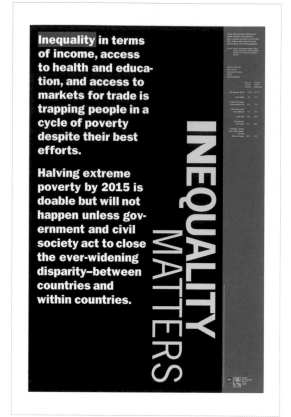
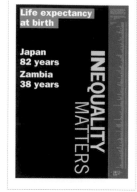
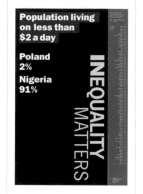

Design is often used not only to promote militaristic causes but also social ones. These posters educate the viewer about the monetary and human costs associated with smoking.
Design: Greteman Group

(Far right) Design informs and educates the public. To create awareness about the effects of music lyrics on abuse toward women, this ad uses popular albums configured as parts of a woman's wardrobe.
Design: Archrival

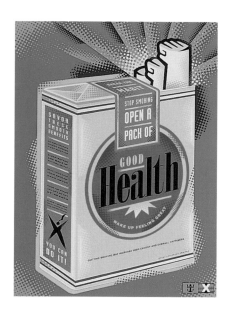

(Opposite page) Work created for nonprofit organizations or done pro bono allows designers creative freedom that can be well worth the sacrifice in pay. And Partners organized an exhibit and fundraiser for the Books for Kids organization, in which some of New York City's most influential designers were asked to create designs that communicated the idea of punctuation. After the exhibit, posters were distributed in design publications and paper promotions.

Michael Beirut

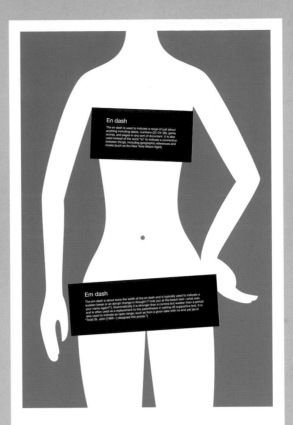

Todd St. John

Stefan Sagmeister

Kent Hunter

Road signs differ from country to country and so does the amount of information the driver is asked to comprehend. In the United States, highway signs are simplified to make navigation easier. In European countries, signage offers more information to the viewer.

The Complete Graphic Designer

Wayfinding

Today, millions of miles of roads connect local communities, cities, and even countries to each other. Therefore, road signs must quickly and effectively communicate directions, regulations, and even warnings to drivers. Language and cultural experience, as well as context, can often exacerbate this problem. The use of semiotics in signage design overcomes these barriers and allows for universal communication.

As the world's population continues to live longer, new challenges such as visibility and readability arise in transportation system design. A study in the United States indicated that by 2005, one-fifth of drivers would be age 65 or older, and recommended that the lettering on highway signs should be as much as 20 percent larger. It also recommended that all current signs be replaced with those that are 40-50 percent larger. To remedy the situation and avoid increasing the size, a new typeface called Clearview Hwy® was developed, featuring larger lowercase letters that are easier to read.

The typeface ClearviewHwy®, was developed to improve legibility of the previous typeface used on highway and directional signage. The new letterforms achieve this through the use of **1** the taller x-height (which allows for wider letters), **2** greater word length, **3** opened up, thinner stroke weight, and **4** the elimination of cut-wedge letters so the lowercase "L" is differentiated from the number "1".

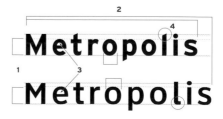

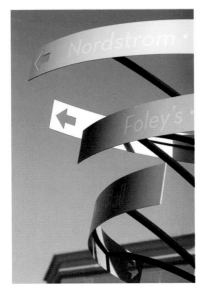

Sometimes, functional design can resemble a piece of art such as this wayfinding pole for a shopping mall. Decorative stones have been affixed to the post, while curvilinear plaques spiral upward from the base. The post is centrally located within a courtyard and each sign points toward a specific destination such as restrooms, an ATM, and Customer Service. Although the piece is beautiful, unlike art its sole purpose is communication.
Design: fd2s

Design for Communication

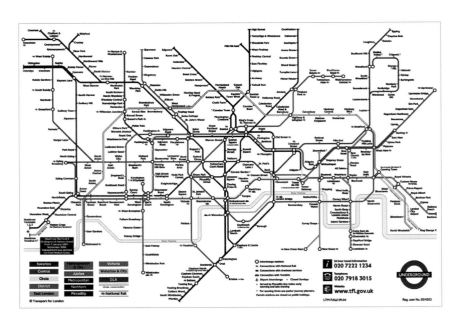

The London subway map is a design classic. The map's simplicity enables users to navigate through the complex network of underground railways that connect various parts of London.

Today, we still communicate through posted imagery and words. Directional signage helps guide people through large buildings as illustrated by this kiosk, which directs the viewer to the appropriate elevator. Modern technology has further enhanced this sign by featuring a call button for assistance.
Design: C&G Partners

ABN·AMRO

DIVERSITY
AND DISABILITY

About 1 in 5 people will
have a mental health issue
at some stage

ABN·AMRO

DIVERSITY
AND RACE

The identity of black
American, Garrett Morgan,
inventor of the traffic light,
is still virtually unknown.

ABN·AMRO

DIVERSITY
AND AGE

The group with the
highest disposable
income in the UK
today are those aged
between 60 and 75

" Design is about getting the right idea,
and getting the idea right."

—Marty Neumeier

Chapter 2: **The**

Design Process

Extraordinary design solutions rarely manifest themselves out of thin air. While it is conceivable that a creative "eureka" can and does take place, it is a rare occurrence; and even then, it takes time for a skilled designer to develop and further refine the idea. More commonly, graphic design is the process of discovering ideas that will enhance the client's image, promote its products or services, or transmit a message that needs to be communicated to the target audience.

The Complete Graphic Designer

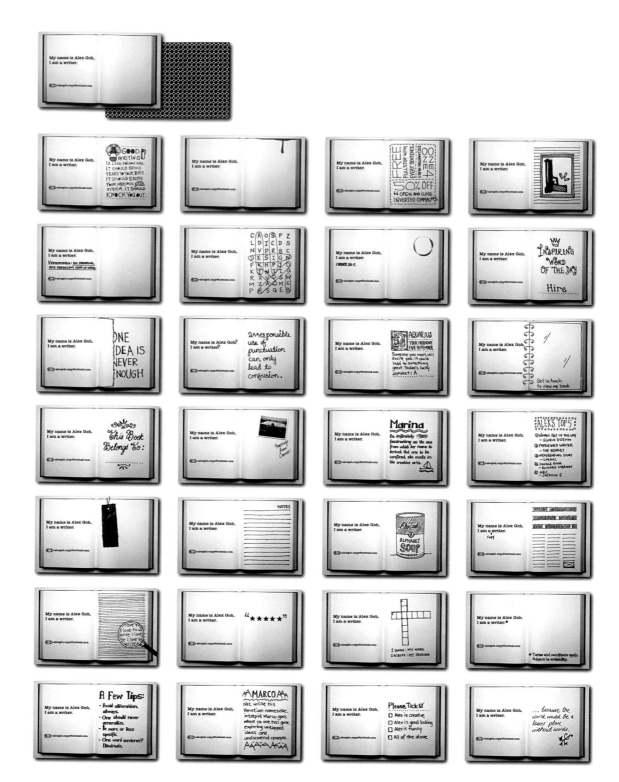

Extraordinary design solutions in which the image, message, and concept
converge are the result of a comprehensive and thorough process of exploration and discovery. To visually communicate the creativity of a copywriter,
this series of business cards uses a photograph of an open book as a
background, with a brief explanation of his services. Doodles and sketches
related to copywriting fill the rest of the card.
Design: Kinetic

By referencing not only the work of an art movement but also incorporating its stylistic conventions, this poster for a Charles Renee Mackintosh exhibit uses typeface, color palette, and imagery to convey an authentic message to viewers.
Design: Shinnoske, Inc.

Although it varies from person to person and from firm to firm, a thoughtful and well-structured design process, like the one we will explore in this chapter, is essential to solving visual communication problems. It is a tried and true methodology for the exploration, experimentation, and, ultimately, discernment of ideas appropriate for the design problem —whether mundane, trite, or cliché, unexpected or out of the ordinary. Referred to as the design concept, the "right" idea is one that is so simple, logical, and relevant to the problem that everything about it communicates the intended message. Good concepts reinforce and drive messages deep into the minds of the target audience.

Visual communication relies on the designer's ability to quickly adapt, understand, and respond to the needs of the client. It is essential to begin by looking at the problem from all angles and then define the most important aspects of that problem. By mapping out these points early on, the designer will be able to generate a variety of appropriate ideas that will quickly help determine the best route to solve a particular design challenge. There are many steps and different ways to work through the design process, and each designer creates a procedure that works best. However, in order to be successful, research, writing, and drawing are all fundamental skills that every designer needs to develop.

Conceptually, this book cover speaks to the audience on many levels. The use of thick black bars are suggestive of the view from inside a prison cell and reinforce the subtitle of the book.
Design: Pentagram

Begin research by answering the following questions about your client:

- What is the client's story or history?

- What are the client's core values that need to be communicated?

- What are the client's unique competitive advantages?

- How does your client differ from his competitors?

- Who is the target audience?

- How will the target audience benefit from the product or service offered?

Research

Conducting research early on is a vital step towards being able to understand and solve visual problems. Thorough exploration of the problem helps designers develop a comprehensive understanding of the client, its goals, and, ultimately, what an appropriate design solution would be. This is especially important when working with a new client or within an unfamiliar industry. To effectively communicate the client's intended message, the designer must gather the information necessary to properly define the problem and generate appropriate ideas.

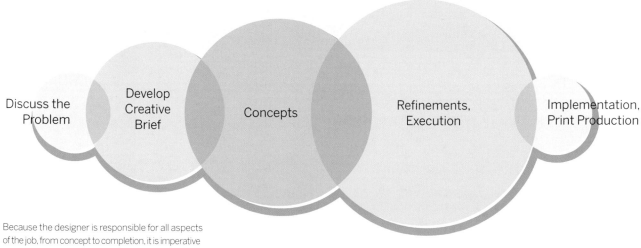

Discuss the Problem

Develop Creative Brief

Concepts

Refinements, Execution

Implementation, Print Production

Because the designer is responsible for all aspects of the job, from concept to completion, it is imperative that he take as much time as necessary to learn the client's business to provide the client with an appropriate and effective design solution.

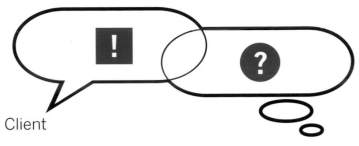

Client

Creative Director

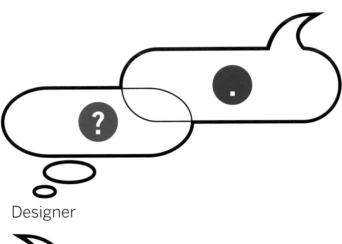

Designer

Establish Credibility with the Client

Becoming a truly valued consultant and indispensable resource to clients should be a priority for every graphic designer. The more a client trusts and respects a designer and his work, the more enjoyable the relationship becomes and the more he will be granted creative freedom. To accomplish this goal, the designer must not only familiarize himself with all aspects of the design business, but must also become an expert in the subject. In addition to being proficient in all aspects of design, the designer must also become intimately familiar with his client's business. A good place to start is with company literature such as annual reports and its website. It is also wise to do some research on the Web to find out how the client is perceived by others and to familiarize yourself with any recent company events. Lastly, numerous trade publications

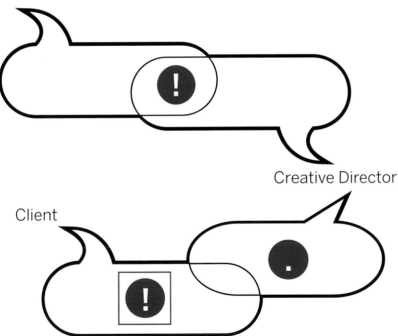

Creative Director

Client

The design process is much like a dialogue between the designer and the client. Typically, the client requests specific design solutions and the designer offers input and suggestions to enhance the client's idea. The resulting solution is often a compromise of ideas that is appropriate for the design problem and meets the client's needs.

1. Take a site tour of the company or organization's facilities. A short visit can provide a wealth of information about its products or services.

2. Interview employees to learn about the company's culture and employee perception. Everyone from senior management to delivery drivers and warehouse staff should be questioned about their role within the company.

3. Examine existing and historical marketing collateral, including annual reports. These are available by request from the Investor Relations department of the company and are sometimes available on its website.

4. Industry or trade magazines offer an abundance of information about a client's target audience as well as insight into the company's competition and market share. These are particularly useful for developing a visual vocabulary of the types of images, graphics, colors, and type styles that are appropriate to the job at hand.

5. The Internet, while convenient and easy to use, should not be the designer's sole source of information because material found online is sometimes inaccurate, biased, or fraudulent.

> " If you want to be a well-paid designer, please the client. If you want to be an award-winning designer, please yourself. If you want to be a great designer, please the audience."
>
> —Unknown

are available and may offer the most important insights into various aspects of the business, providing the designer with an indispensable perspective. Research allows the designer to truly understand and establish credibility with the client, and to develop the vernacular to speak intelligently about what the company does, how it does it, and why it matters to its customers.

Conduct Internal Meetings and Interviews

Informational meetings are face-to-face discussions that may include employees at some or all levels of the organization. These interviews will allow the designer to gain insight into internal procedures, processes, and the client in general. This is a good opportunity to get the client to define the company's mission, history, and essential qualities that need to be conveyed in the design solution, as well as to define the target audience and goals for the piece being created. Do not be afraid to ask questions; assumptions make the designer look both arrogant and unsympathetic to the client's needs and can result in costly and time-consuming mistakes. In every interaction with the client, express genuine interest in the subject matter and demonstrate the desire to be a valuable marketing partner. This will quickly establish trust and enable the client to speak freely and confidently about the task at hand.

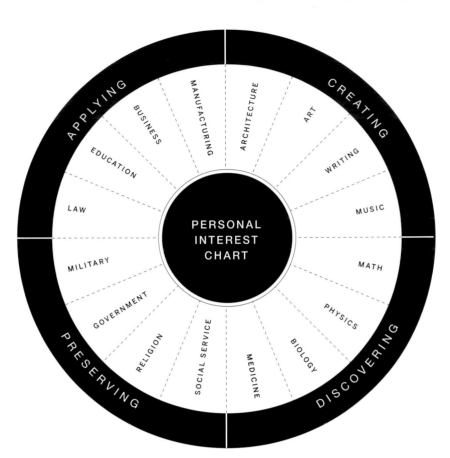

The goals for a design project depend not only on the needs and expectations of the target audience, but also the client's industry. Design that is appropriate for one type of business might not be for others. There are four main market segments and industry types represented—those next to each other on the chart have similar preferences in terms of acceptable imagery, color schemes, and graphics, while those directly opposite often have conflicting interests. Being sensitive to the unique preferences of these interest groups enables the designer to create more effective design solutions.
Design: Marty Neumeier

Define the Needs of the Target Audience

Researching the needs and expectations of the target audience allows for the creation of memorable solutions that effectively communicate a company's core values, attributes, or unique messages. Informal discussions with current or potential customers will provide useful insight and help determine any positive or negative perceptions about the company, its product, or services that may inform or become part of the final visual solution.

Design is a multi-tiered language, so defining the means of the message (type, color, layout, and imagery) is an important part of the final work. Effectively communicating

with the target audience depends upon the development of a visual vocabulary that appeals to the sensibilities of the viewer. To get a clear understanding of what the target audience will respond to, look at all aspects of their lives, from jobs to hobbies and interests. Demographics such as age, gender, income level, and education are equally important considerations. Begin by collecting and analyzing magazines, books, or examples of marketing materials that address the specific interests of the target audience. This will help define appropriate design choices such as color, typography, and the overall feel of a layout. It is also important to think about how the piece will be used. Does the design need to be eye-catching or does it contain a lot of important information that

needs to be clearly organized? Remember that communicating is first and foremost, so never let the design stand in the way of getting your message across.

Defining the Problem

Comprehensive and exhaustive research will enable the designer to clearly define a visual problem. Once the designer has completed this step, it is wise to present his findings to the client to confirm that his information is accurate and his design plan is in keeping with the client's vision. Research thus becomes the rationale for finding the design solution that will be the most appropriate for the problem.

Creative agencies or firms develop their own creative procedures. Depending on the size and scope of a project or the number of individuals immersed in the problem, the design process may be more involved. Clearly communicating this process with clients at the beginning of a project informing them of the complexities inherent in solving visual problems will not only make them feel more involved and vested in the process, but will also result in a smoother relationship.
Design: Willoughby Design

(Opposite page) The creative brief offers insight into the successful attributes of an organization's identity or marketing collateral. Comparing those with competing organizations allows for the development of a unique solution to a visual problem.
Design: Indicia Design

The Complete Graphic Designer

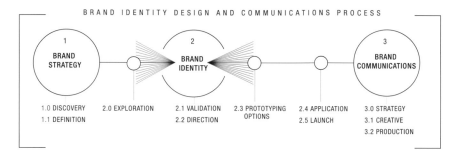

BRAND IDENTITY DESIGN AND COMMUNICATIONS PROCESS

Developing the Creative Brief

Designers are given specific visual problems to solve that must meet defined business objectives, be delivered within budget, and work within a myriad of other possible constraints. These problems can range in scope from designing brochures or other marketing collateral to developing an extensive corporate identity for a company. Sometimes, however, visual problems and their goals may be more challenging; for example, the company may be trying to increase their market share or appeal to an entirely dif-

ferent audience than they have in the past. In these cases, it is vital to have a thorough brief that clearly outlines the parameters. In some cases, clients are not familiar with what a brief needs to address and will unknowingly provide the designer with an incomplete brief or vague goals. In this situation, it is the designer's responsibility to lead the client in developing a creative brief that outlines the task at hand and provides a framework the designer can work within.

Because many design problems have multiple phases or parts to the final solution, the creative brief should include a detailed timeline for the project. Creating a visual "map" of dates for deliverables keeps everyone involved on the same page and the project on schedule.
Design: Dean Olufson

Evaluation of the current "Friends" Logo

The current Friends of Battered Women and Their Children logo is shown above. Compared to other logos of similar organizations, the "Friends" logo is very plain, and looks out of date. The stylized figures of the woman and her two children are reminiscent of the Modernist design aesthetic of the 1960s and 1970s.

Further dating the current logo design is the typeface used for the organization's name—called "Hobo". This font is far too comical and whimsical, and does not project a serious or professional image for the organization. While longevity is important in any identity redesign, this is clearly a design that is past due for an update.

In addition to updating the current "Friends" identity, it is important to consider flexibility of the mark—a logo must be designed to be versatile for use in all applications, including apparel, print collateral, and on screen. The current logo is too horizontal in format, which limits its application to collateral. In the example below, when the current logo is reduced to 1.5" wide, it becomes almost illegible and completely unreadable. The same result happens when the logo is viewed from a distance (such as on a billboard, etc.).

2

Between Friends Identity

For the Between Friends identity project, Indicia Design examined the provided creative brief as well as the background information provided. From this information, we determined that there were basically three different approaches that we could take when developing our solution. They are as follows:

Approach 1: Caring; Shelter, Support

"Between Friends" provides a safe haven and shelter for those women or individuals who are victims of domestic violence. They provide healing and nurturing, as well as caring, through education they prevent further abuse.

Possible images explored for this approach include: hearts, holding hands, hugs, a fence (protection), a house or home, people, a welcome mat, etc.

Approach 2: Life change, freedom

"Between Friends" empowers individuals to rise above their abuse and move on with their lives by motivating them to take control again.

Possible images explored for this approach include: arms thrown up (crossing a finish line), jumping for joy, untying bonds, letting loose, chains breaking, the idea of growth, and the idea of renewal.

Approach 3: Hope, Optimism

"Between Friends" offers a new start for victims by nurturing victims who have "come into the light", so to speak...

Possible images explored for this approach include: candle, sunshine, rays of light, a globe, the idea of something rough that gets refined or smoother, the idea of growth, the idea of the changing of seasons (springtime), and the idea of renewal.

The following pages contain our best ideas and concepts for the new Between Friends logo. Please keep in mind that these are pretty rough ideas, so if you enjoy one particular concept but would like to see it rendered differently, that is something that can be achieved. Following these concepts we have included all of our preliminary work, so you can get a sense for how we arrived at the concepts presented.

Next Steps: Please select three of the following concepts that you would like for us to refine and present as computer generated roughs, including final type treatments, etc. Should you have any questions, please feel free to call us at (816) 471–6200.

Components of a Creative Brief

The creative brief is much like a road map for success in solving a graphic design problem and as such, is an invaluable resource for the designer. Every creative brief should contain the following information:

1. General parameters
What is the budget? What are the deadlines? What are the deliverables?

2. The specific problem that needs to be solved
Is it a direct mail piece, a website, or a corporate identity that needs to be created?

3. A brief overview of the organization
What do they do? How long have they been in business? Where are they located? Who is the specific person the designer will be working with?

4. A list of business and design objectives
What is the client trying to accomplish through the design piece(s) being created?

5. The target audience and demographic information
What are the gender, age range, education, income levels, hobbies, and preferences of the target audience? What type of visual imagery do they respond to?

6. The unique attributes of the product(s) or service(s) the company offers
What are customers' perceptions (positive or negative)? Why would the target audience choose this particular product or service over its competitors?

7. The competition
What are the competing companies, products, or services? What strengths and weaknesses should be discussed? Compile a comparative study of websites that illustrates the visual vocabulary of imagery that will resonate with the target audience.

8. Creative approach
What is the visual problem and what are the steps the designer will take to solve it?

USI Industrial Services: Brochure Concepts

1 | Your Lifeline

Concept: Driven by safety and a commitment to each client's needs and services, USI is a partner and lifeline for its clients' plant maintenance and construction. USI works to build true, collaborative partnerships that respond efficiently and safely to clients' needs whether those revolve around planned turnarounds, routine maintenance, or emergency responses.

2 | Behind the Scenes

Concept: USI's goal is *not* to be noticed, to work seamlessly within its clients' operation and needs to ensure that plant operations continue smoothly and safely. With its dependable, reliable, and knowledgeable staff, USI makes sure the work gets done to its clients' satisfaction. Planned turnaround or unplanned maintenance, USI is there, putting the clients and their operations first.

3 | Roots

Concept: USI may be a new company, but its expertise is rooted in our employees' years of experience and expertise, in the field and with similar clients and services. That history and our ability not just to follow but to lead tradition allows USI to provide services to the construction and plant maintenance industry with a combination of excellence, innovation, and passion.

Concepts for a company brochure are explored first in writing. In this case, the design firm worked with a copywriter to develop ideas, and then provided short descriptions of each idea to the client for review. Generally, once a client signs off on an idea, the designer will further refine it and create or commission visuals, such as photography and illustration, to communicate the concept.
Design: Indicia Design

Concept Development

Developing concepts, the most important part of any design project, occurs in the mind, not on a computer screen. During this crucial phase of the design process, the designer should spend his time generating ideas away from the computer. Thoroughly analyzing design problems through writing exercises allows the designer to later translate abstract ideas or rough concepts into poignant visuals that will connect with the target audience and deliver its message.

The Designer as Writer

Using the written word, the designer combines fragments of thoughts or ideas into refined concepts. It is often easier to think about complex or abstract ideas in words that will provide clues as to how to solve a design problem by using visual symbols and metaphors. The more literate and articulate the designer, the more prolific he will be in producing original ideas; many top art directors at creative agencies have roots in copywriting or journalism because of their ability to capture the essence of an idea in as few words as possible.

Idea Incubation

Brainstorming is the process of generating ideas as quickly as possible. Write down every idea that comes to mind, no matter how silly or irrelevant it may seem, because it may later influence or spark a great idea. Design is the process of eliminating ineffective ideas or concepts in order to narrow the possibilities to a few strong ones. The following techniques will aid designers in generating unique design concepts:

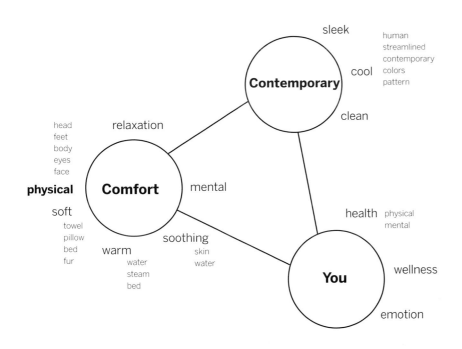

sleek

human
streamlined
contemporary
colors
pattern

cool

Contemporary

clean

relaxation

head
feet
body
eyes
face

physical

Comfort

mental

soft

towel
pillow
bed
fur

soothing

warm

water
steam
bed

skin
water

health   physical
            mental

You

wellness

emotion

The creation of an idea tree helps when brainstorming concepts for visual solutions. Core ideas are connected to related words, thoughts, or phrases to visually portray stream-of-consciousness thinking.
Design: Indicia Design

1. Stream of consciousness/free association

Write down any word that comes to mind when thinking about the subject matter including emotions, colors, perceptions, or phrases; anything and everything is appropriate. Revisit this list of thoughts later to eliminate some of the unusable ideas. This technique allows for unfettered thought.

2. Create an idea tree

Idea trees give visual structure to stream of consciousness idea generation. Thoughts flow in a logical progression as each idea builds off of the previous one—ideas are placed onto a page with related words "branching" off of them. To get started, write down the subject matter (the company or product name might also be appropriate) within a circle. All related thoughts connected with that idea are written down with lines connecting each to the previous idea. Repeat this process for each word until the ideas become very specific or no longer relate to the subject matter.

3. Use a dictionary and thesaurus

Due to their descriptive nature, word definitions give the designer visual clues for possible solutions. In addition to helping understand terminology used by the client, the dictionary is an indispensable tool for translating written ideas into visual symbols and metaphors. Write down the definition for each word from the free association or the idea tree exercise. Underline particularly descriptive words or phrases within each definition, and write those words out on the same sheet of paper with their definitions. Next, use a thesaurus to find related words or synonyms.

4. Combine unlikely ideas

The Latin word for thinking is "cogitate," which literally translated means "to mix together." Taking two ideas or words from the designer's brainstorming exercises and combining them together often yields unexpected and surprising results. Paul Rand was a huge proponent of this method of generating ideas, referring to it as "combinatory play." He believed that the more childlike a designer could think by combining two or more ideas, the more unique and creative a solution would be developed, particularly during the sketching phase of the design process.

When designing a spread, sketches prove useful for determining the position of elements such as headlines and visuals on the page. Unless an image is an integral part of the page layout (i.e. text that wraps around or interacts with an image), its placement may be represented by a box with an "X" through it as a placeholder.
Design: Indicia Design

Visualizing Ideas

Drawing is essential to solving design problems since ideas must be translated from written form into images that communicate with the audience. Because of this, drawing is a fundamental skill that every designer must possess and cultivate. Putting pen to paper should be the first step in the development process because it allows one to recreate what one sees as well as explore perceived shapes, line, form, texture, tonal value, depth, and color. Sketching also allows the designer and client to envision the final design solution prior to executing or producing a finished design.

Sketching is part of the process designers use to visualize and explore various concepts. Quick thumbnail sketches allow them to quickly ascertain which are the best ideas and which elements, such as perspective, subject matter, and composition, need to be addressed before presenting concepts to the client or moving to the computer for rendering or refinement. While most designers use computer applications such as Adobe® Photoshop®, InDesign®, and Illustrator® to execute their ideas, simply having these proficiencies does not make a good designer. A solid concept is the necessary foundation of any good design.

Thumbnail sketches quickly help the designer validate an idea. In these sketches for a layout, the approximate proportions of the piece and image placement are explored. Sketches do not need intricate detail and use annotations to further expand upon the idea.
Design: Indicia Design

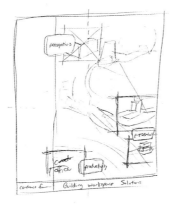
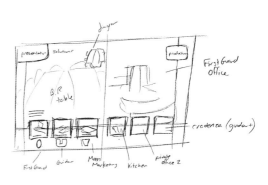

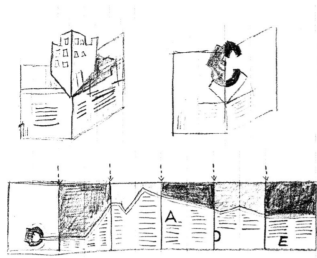

Thumbnails not only determine the placement of design elements, they also help determine how a dimensional piece will be constructed, as with these brochure concepts.
Design: Indicia Design

Thumbnails

Thumbnail sketches are small, roughly drawn visuals created in rapid succession. Form, composition, spatial relationships, text placement, and even graphic treatments are investigated to analyze whether or not an idea is working or if further studies are needed. Sometimes several sketches must be drawn to find a workable solution, requiring dozens, if not hundreds, of thumbnails for critique. Even so, thumbnails make it possible to determine the validity of an idea much faster than searching for the perfect image, scanning and manipulating it using the computer, and placing it into a design, only to find the idea is an inappropriate direction. Experimentation through sketching is an essential component of designing strong work, and the time invested up front always saves the designer time overall.

In developing the logo for Lincoln Park Zoo's 10th Anniversary "Jammin' at the Zoo," the designer executed these tight pencil sketches to explore various concepts for the mark, including typographic solutions and the use of different animals and musical instruments.
Design: Fernandez Design

In creating a new brand image for Sheridan's Lattés and Frozen Custard, a brand positioning statement was developed by the creative team.
Design: Willoughby Design

Selling the Idea

Presenting ideas to the client for feedback is the next crucial step in the design process. The designer must be able to not only speak intelligently about her work and the rationale behind it (if a creative brief is followed, the design will meet the client's goals and objectives), she must also be able to prove that the visual solution works. To generate excitement, acceptance, and approval, ideas must be refined and executed in full-color, rendered mockups that help clients visualize the final design solution. If a solution involves special print processes or unique execution, the designer must not only explore the feasibility and costs of producing such a design, but must provide samples as well.

Presenting Design Solutions

Client presentations are a delicate balancing act for the designer because aesthetics and practicality converge when executing design solutions. The desire to produce ground-breaking and award-winning work sometimes conflicts with the business objectives of the client and the needs of its audience. As a result, the graphic designer should strive to produce and present the client with ideas that will satisfy everyone.

Time and budget allowing, present at least three fully rendered and executed ideas for client feedback and critique: a conservative solution that works well with existing collateral and reflects the design sensibilities of the client, an innovative and extreme design that pushes the client's budget and aesthetic, and a blend of those two options. Do not present too many options because it makes the client's decision-making more difficult and sometimes results in a design that incorporates elements from several ideas into one, thus watering down the effectiveness of the original design. Be sure to present samples of any specialty paper, inks, or unique finishes you are considering.

Executing the Concept or Idea

Once the research and concept development phases have been completed, it is time to turn to the details. Whereas pencil sketches allow ideas to be quickly produced and analyzed, executing a final design concept requires careful attention to choreographing the design elements to work in concert and communicate the intended message. Equally important is that the design can be reproduced on a mass scale. No matter how creative or innovative a design solution is, if it is unable to be mass-produced within budget the design completely

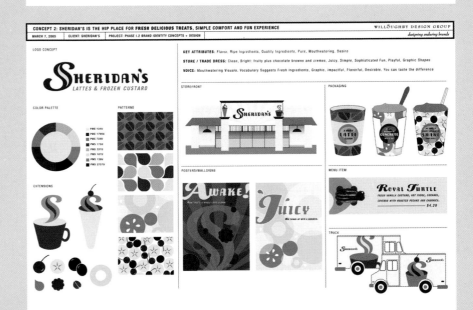

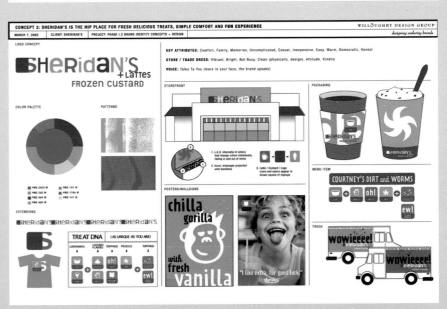

Each of the three original concepts presented to Sheridan's Lattés and Frozen Custard conveys the core values of the brand strategy brief through visuals that appeal to the target audience, including color palettes, patterns, and designs for store signage and collateral.

Design: Willoughby Design

The Design Process

fails to solve the client's visual problem. So determining this early on is imperative.

Most designers execute final designs on the computer because it allows them to quickly and easily explore variations and create final reproduction art. The proficient designer uses applications to his advantage to quickly render computer generated "roughs" for the client. Adobe® Photoshop® is a leading image manipulation and editing tool; Illustrator® is ideal for creating vector artwork such as logos or single page documents; and InDesign® is a page layout and design program for longer publications.

When executing a design, practical aspects of a project such as printing processes or distribution methods must be addressed. Contact local printers to receive print estimates. Well-developed prototypes or sketches of the piece, including paper selection and printing techniques, better enable the printer to deliver a price that meets the client's budget. If mailing is required, the designer should verify postage rates with the post office and confirm that no extra postage will be required.

Executing a logo solution requires the exploration of several variations on a single idea. In these examples, refined concepts are shown with the final client-approved mark.
Design: Gardner Design

Presentation Tips

Presenting ideas to a client, especially for the first time, can be a nerve-wracking experience for the graphic designer. After hours or days of work, the designer and client meet face-to-face, sometimes in the presence of a committee, to discuss the thought process that is explored through the visual problem. Designs are presented for review and feedback. Here are some steps that will ensure a successful and productive client presentation:

1. Neatness counts

Items arranged on presentation boards should be mounted straight or in consistent locations across multiple boards—pieces mounted at different angles become a focal point for the client and distract from the presentation. Likewise, pencil marks or excess glue should be removed from all boards.

2. Provide samples of unique materials or printing techniques

If a design utilizes unique printing techniques, such as metallic inks, varnishes, die cuts or embossing, provide a sample of the technique. For folding pieces or multi-page documents, create a mockup or prototype that will allow the client to visualize what the final piece will look like.

3. Be confident

Approach each meeting as the design expert. Be prepared to answer questions and explain the thought process behind a design. Speak articulately and with proper grammar.

4. Be prepared

Bring a writing utensil, notepad, and the job jacket to the meeting. Have all process work available to show as rationale for the design solution presented.

5. Show only the best ideas

Never bring to a meeting work you would not like to see chosen because it just may be selected. Show your preferred choice first.

6. Show alternative options, not variations of a single idea

Clients want a few options from which to choose, so showing a similar design concept that is merely rendered in three different color schemes or with few major changes is not satisfactory.

7. Don't overwhelm them

Showing too many options makes selecting a final option very difficult. Three or four distinct directions are appropriate.

8. Help in the decision-making process

Elevating the design sensibilities of clients is an important aspect of the graphic design process—this is why a professional was hired in the first place. If the client hesitates or has difficultly selecting a design concept, lead him to choose the most appropriate design solution. If a project is a collaborative effort involving multiple designers, be sure all the designers agree on the best solution and be firm about that choice.

To showcase the staccato spot-less printing technique—a new method of offset lithography that eliminates halftone dot patterns—this brochure features large areas of solid colors that are built using the four process colors. Colorful imagery and graphics further illustrate the color reproduction accuracy.
Design: Design Raymann

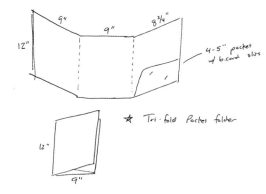

Providing illustrations or mock-ups helps the printer estimate a print job and enables the designer to develop final print-ready artwork that meets the required measurements.

Print Process Considerations

Regardless of how innovative, inspiring, or creative a design solution may be, if it is unable to be reproduced on a mass scale and within a client's budget, the design has failed. There are several printing methods including offset lithography, letterpress, and silk-screening. How the piece will be distributed or transmitted, the materials it will be printed on, any unique finishing techniques, and the look of the piece will all be considered when determining which printing method will yield the best results.

Offset Lithography

This is the most common method of reproducing artwork. Printing presses come in a variety of sizes, can print onto single sheets or continuous rolls of paper, and allow for multiple colors. Full-color reproduction is achieved through the use of the four process colors (cyan, magenta, yellow, and black); how the colors overlap determines the final color. Offset lithography is the least expensive way to print quantities of 500 to 100,000 pieces. Offset presses print at 150-300 lpi (lines per inch, equivalent to 300 and 600 dpi, respectively).

Letterpress

Letterpress was the most popular form of printing until the 1960s when offset presses began to replace them. In this traditional print process, ink is rolled onto a metal or wood plate and is then pressed into a sheet of paper. Due to the amount of pressure applied, letterpress often flattens out the paper in the areas where ink is applied, giving a very tactile quality

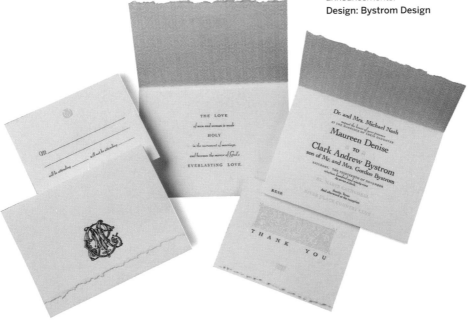

Using the letterpress as a printing method gives pieces a hand-made quality and evokes a classic elegance, especially for formal invitations or announcements.
Design: Bystrom Design

to a piece. Thick pieces of paper or cardboard may be printed using this technique, but only one color at a time may be printed. Most letterpress presses still in existence are used for high-quality, specialty pieces such as invitations. Letterpress typically uses transparent, solid areas of color ink, as it cannot accommodate percentages of color.

Silk Screen

When permanence is an issue or unusual materials must be used in a design, silk-screen presses are very versatile methods of reproduction. They print on almost any kind of substrate material, including metal or fabric, and can even be applied to dimensional objects. Solid, opaque ink is applied to a surface by using a squeegee to push ink through a meshed screen. T-shirts, ceramics, and plastics are all appropriate for silk-screen printing. Depending on the material being printed, halftone dot patterns should be very coarse (no more than 60 lpi).

Vinyl Applications

Much interior signage is reproduced using adhesive vinyl lettering, which is cut into thin sheets of plastic vinyl using a computer-directed blade. The back is adhe-

In addition to its unusual format, this brochure and pocket folder are silk screened on a natural-colored, uncoated stock. When designing a work that will be silk screened, it is best to use solid colors and 100 percent of a hue rather than a percentage or tint (tints do not reproduce well due to coarse line screens and large dot patterns). Thin strokes and intricate detail are also difficult to reproduce with this technique.
Design: Indicia Design

Plastic paper with a dull finish was used with a black foil stamp to create a striking tone-on-tone effect for this brochure cover.
Design: Late Night Creative

Window graphics such as these were created using vinyl-cut graphics that are then applied to the inside face of the glass. Only solid color graphics may be used, a limitation the designer should be aware of.
Design: Gardner Design

sive-coated so that it may be applied onto smooth surfaces such as plastic, glass, or metal. Vehicle graphics, interior signage, and window decals are all vinyl-cut letters. Vinyl comes in large sheets of pre-selected solid colors (you cannot specify a CMYK or Pantone color). Additionally, gradations and tints are not possible.

Paper Selection

Choosing the right paper for a visual problem is extremely important to the overall concept and execution of a printed piece. Clients depend on the designer to recommend the most appropriate paper for a design project. Papers are not just a surface on which to lay ink, they should also enhance the design. In addition to how a piece will ultimately be used or distributed, the designer must also consider the paper's weight, color, texture, and whether to use coated or uncoated stock.

Most printers keep both coated and uncoated paper stock in their inventory so they are immediately available for printing. Known as "house sheets," these papers are bought in bulk at reduced prices, thus decreasing the overall cost of a print job. Even though paper comes in a staggering variety of textures, colors, and finishes, a printer's selection of readily available stock is sometimes limited. Consult with the printer or a paper company representative for a wider selection of choices.

Coated Paper

Coated paper has a smooth surface and special coating that results in more accurate and vibrant color, crisper images, and sharper detail. It is an ideal choice for pieces that incorporate photography, vivid color, or require a high-end, finished feel such as magazines or trade publications. Brochures, catalogs, and sales sheets are often printed

To promote the specialty papers available from a paper company, this invitation uses spot color printing on cotton paper. The 100 percent cotton envelopes are translucent, allowing the typography and stylized imagery to show through.
Design: Dotzero Design

on coated stock because color accuracy is imperative to sales. Although widely popular for most print jobs, it is not appropriate for all types of print jobs—the special coating has a tendency to ruin office equipment that uses a heat transfer process, such as laser printers or copiers, and is difficult to write on using a ballpoint pen or pencil.

Uncoated Paper

Uncoated stock has a more pronounced grain or texture that allows ink to soak into the paper, thus muting colors and creating a "softer" appearance. Depending upon the job, this can be a positive or negative quality, so take this into careful consideration. Uncoated stock is appropriate for designs that require a personal, elegant, or sophisticated look, such as invitations, announcements, and personal stationery. Some print processes, such as letterpress or silk screening, are most effective when used on uncoated stock. Both coated and uncoated papers are available in numerous colors including many degrees of whiteness.

Specialty Paper

Specialty papers include, but are certainly not limited to, translucent sheets, cast-coated sheets with mirror-like finishes, recycled papers, and textured stocks. When used to enhance the concept of a visual solution, specialty papers are extremely effective; if they are used as a gimmick, they waste the client's money. These papers are more costly to produce and more susceptible to trends so are often only available for a limited time. Additionally, they must be ordered in large quantities from the paper mill, adding more production time to the print job.

If unsure about what type of paper is most appropriate for the print job, consult with the printer for recommendations or request samples from paper companies and distributors. Their knowledgeable representatives will discuss the strengths and weaknesses of each of their lines.

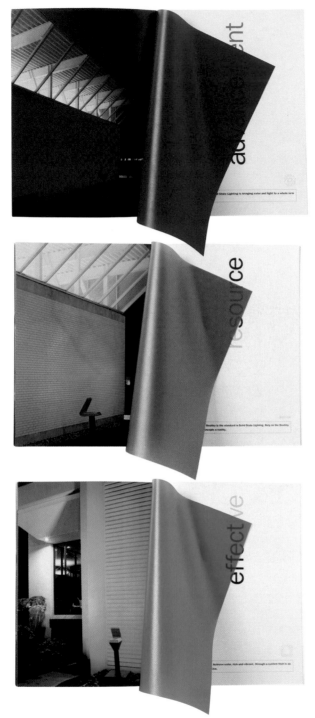

Colored translucent paper conceals and then
reveals the benefits of using outdoor lighting
products. As visible light consists of red, green,
and blue rays, these colors were used in this piece
to effectively reinforce the concept of lighting.
Design: SamataMason

Finishing Techniques

Unique finishing techniques, such
as die cutting, embossing, or adding foils or varnishes, can greatly
enhance the execution of a printed
piece. Die-cut windows hide and
then reveal an image, thus promoting user interaction, while unusually
shaped collateral surprises and en-
gages the viewer. Emphasizing certain elements of a design through
embossing (raised impressions in
the paper), metallic foil, or varnishes
(clear coats of ink that add touches
of high gloss or dullness to a design) are all enhancements that may
be made to a final printed piece. It
is important to remember, however,
that these details are only truly effective when they help to reinforce
the overall concept. These details
alone will not improve a piece that
is weak in concept or execution;
they will just make it more expensive to produce.

For this high-end CEO Summit piece for Nokia, the design firm utilized several finishing techniques such as die cutting the event logo out of the box slip cover, designing a uniquely shaped program and itinerary that is bound using wire-o® techniques, and choosing a custom printed binder for the event collateral.
Design: Yellow Octopus

Keeping a Design Process Record

Design is often a compromise of ideas between the designer and clients, so sometimes the best solution is not selected for final implementation and print production. Maintaining records of the design process, whether in a job jacket or sketchbook, preserves the evolution of ideas and creates a place for unused ones to be cataloged for future use. Process cataloging is also invaluable for resolving billing or ownership disputes such as proving the amount of work that was put into a project or when a design was first created.

Remember that good design connects with an intended audience. Developing a well-researched creative brief, adhering to the guidelines set within, and communicating with the client will ensure that only successful concepts and solutions are produced and that precious time is not wasted on ineffective concepts.

A complex and intricate blind emboss is used to convey the idea of a sidewalk that has been decorated with names while the cement was still wet. Embossing is a subtle technique whose tactile qualities engage the senses and enhance the overall impact of a piece.
Design: And Partners

Sometimes a composition will
use several grids layered on top of
each other or at different angles.
Design: Fauxpas Grafik

Gridlines are not only visible in this
composition, but act as the illustrated
portion of the poster, launching a new
corporate identity.
Design: Templin Brink

Chapter 3: **Page Layout and Design**

A painter works with a brush on canvas, a sculptor, a chisel and stone, and a graphic designer, a computer and a blank page. While the fine artist typically has a personal opinion or expression they want to display, the designer must conjure up a way to display someone else's message and also have it resonate with the intended audience. Printed collateral for mass reproduction and consumption is the product of concept development, composition, and creative execution. To this end, page layout and design are fundamental skills the designer must master in order to create effective work.

This promotional pocket folder for Pitney Bowes uses blind embossing of mail-related indicia on the outside of the cover and a unique pocket in front for the brochure. The brochure itself is very clean and corporate with strong visual images, bold colors, and simple graphics. **Design: And Partners**

The Complete Graphic Designer

Page layout is a general term used to describe the look and feel of any printed piece of communication that is designed to solve a visual problem. These solutions can come in various sizes and shapes. From simple postcards, one-page pamphlets, and sales sheets to oversize posters, multipage brochures, and books, it is a designer's responsibility to determine and create an effective visual translation of the client's message. The wide-spread availability and popularity of page-layout software has created an entire industry of nonprofessional desktop publishers who know how to use the computer programs, and have limited knowledge of typography and page layout, but do not necessarily have the talent or eye for good design. The true graphic designer has a thorough understanding of the field to determine the most effective design for his client's needs, and the experience to educate the client about the intricacies of page layout and design.

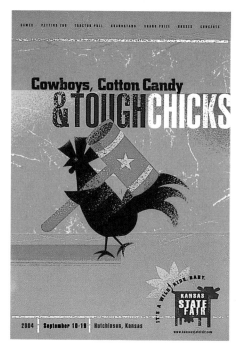

A simple composition with bright colors, dominant elements, and a clear message makes this poster stand out from others. **Design: Greteman Group**

The playful use of typography can add visual interest to a page layout, especially when mixed with the dramatic use of color and imagery.
Design: Greteman Group

Vivid imagery combined with nostalgic images draws upon the history and tradition of Plum Creek Golf Course. Old West-style headings and initial caps reinforce the heritage of the converted horse farm.
Design: Lodge Design

The basics of page layout should accommodate adequate white space and margins to allow for easy reading and comprehension. Text should not be placed too close to the gutter. In the event that a headline or piece of text does need to span the spread, have the space between words cross the gutter or loosen kerning between letters within the word.
Design: SamataMason

TIR DESTINY Design for the future of light. The art of Solid State Lighting (SSL). TIR's Destiny Series of products embodies functionality, style and quality. Destiny exemplifies the philosophy of superb design. Destiny products are engineered to specification grade quality. High output performance with mainstream capability. Destiny products are specialized tools for specific lighting applications for modeling and accentuating architectural forms with colored or color-changing light.

The Complete Graphic Designer

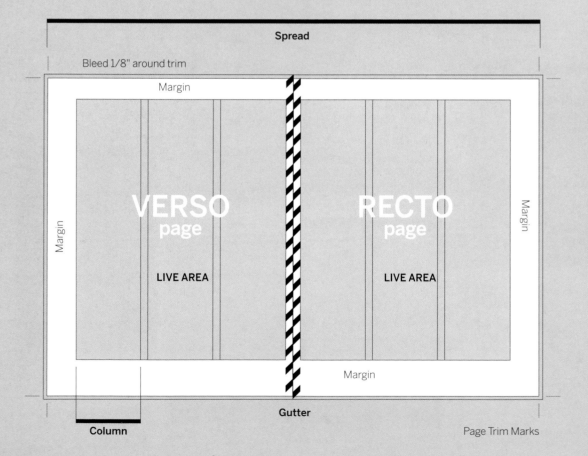

Spread

Bleed 1/8" around trim

Margin

Margin

VERSO page

RECTO page

Margin

LIVE AREA

LIVE AREA

Gutter

Margin

Column

Page Trim Marks

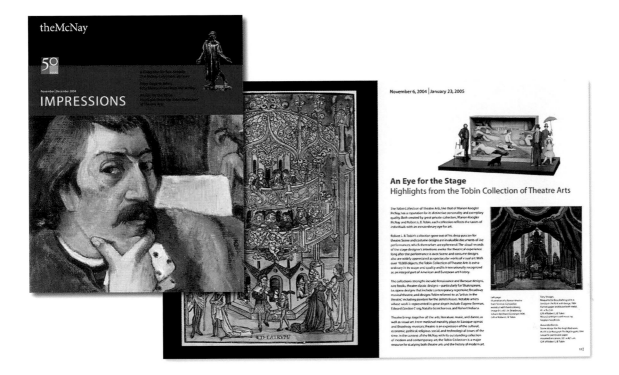

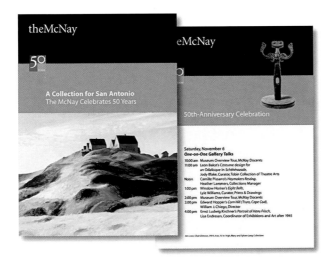

Brochures redesigned for the Marion Koogler McNay Art Museum in San Antonio, Texas, use a simple grid structure to achieve consistency among the museum's collateral. The grid may be used with one, two, or four columns of text.
Design: C&G Partners

Page Layout & Design

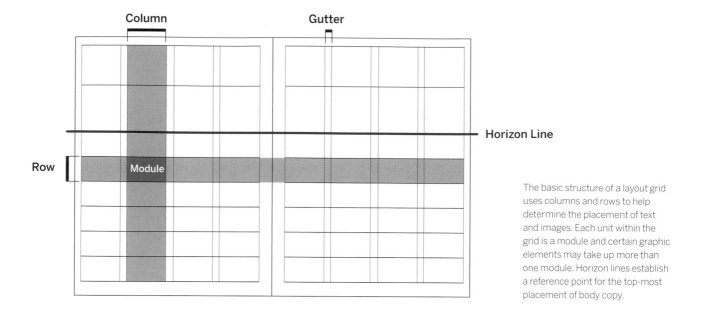

Column

Gutter

Horizon Line

Row

Module

The basic structure of a layout grid uses columns and rows to help determine the placement of text and images. Each unit within the grid is a module and certain graphic elements may take up more than one module. Horizon lines establish a reference point for the top-most placement of body copy.

The Grid

Confronting a blank page on which to design a layout is a daily challenge for graphic designers, one that often intimidates even the most seasoned professional. There are hundreds, if not thousands, of design possibilities. Complicating matters further, most projects have multiple pages or spreads that require continuity throughout the document or publication. To meet this challenge head on, designers should employ the use of grids.

The grid is an invisible framework of guides used to construct a page layout or composition for a printed piece. They give structure to the page and help ensure consistency across the document. By having text line up at the same point on every page, maintaining column widths, aligning images with text or other images,

and placing page numbers in the same spot throughout, there is an orderly rationale for the design. Text and images are not dropped haphazardly onto the page or collaged together, but are placed within different grid "modules" that guide the viewer's eyes through the document, which makes for easy comprehension.

Grids may span an entire spread and divide it evenly into modules. Grids sometimes exist only within the live area of a layout as defined by ample white space or the margins around them. The size and number of grid modules at the designer's disposal are completely arbitrary. The purpose of creating a grid is to give order to the composition. The more grid modules used, the greater the possibilities.

There are times when it is appropriate to break the rules of the grid in design, but this must be well thought out to be effective. In this case, to illustrate the concept of creative inspiration, or making the "right brain heavier," the designer has rotated the text of the poster to give the illusion that the right side of each copy block is being weighed down.
Design: Kinetic

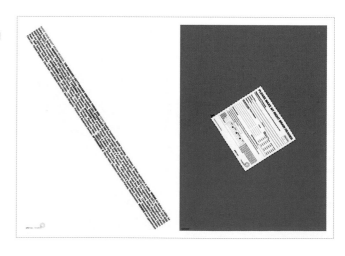

This fold out poster/brochure for a chess tournament uses a simple three-column grid with clearly defined grid modules to organize text and images. Large amounts of white space and colored text help guide the viewer's eyes around the page and disseminate information about the event.
Design: CDT Design

Sometimes a composition will use several grids layered on top of each other. For these Nature Museum posters, grids have been rotated off axis to help accentuate and highlight important information.
Design: Fauxpas Grafik

These grid structures have been created using the Fibonacci sequence of numbers and the golden ratio, both of which are naturally occurring phenomenon.

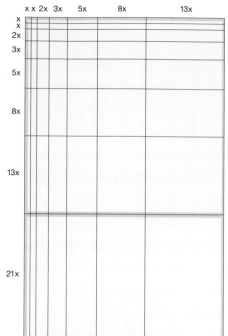

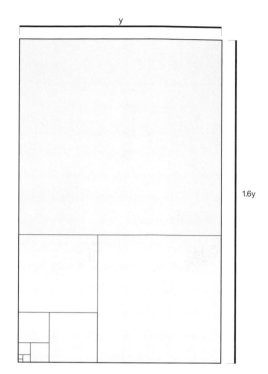

URED OVLAŠTENOG ARHITEKTA

The golden ratio is not only found in nature, but is used in classical architecture as well. For this logo for a small architecture firm, the golden ratio has been used to create a well-structured and proportional mark.
Design: Ideo/Croatia

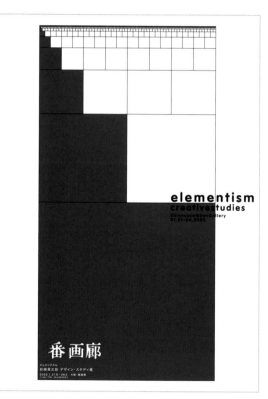

The composition of this poster uses a well-defined grid based on the golden ratio. Each element, from the main title of the piece to the supporting copy, lines up with the grid lines.
Design: Shinnoske, Inc.

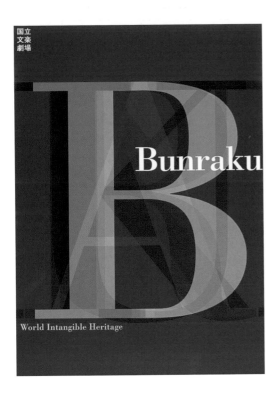

In some instances, typography is used as an illustration, as in these layouts. Letterforms overlap to form surprising new shapes and unique color combinations.
Design: Shinnoske, Inc.

Page Elements

Typography

Graphic designers should embody a love and passion for typography—not only for the way in which letters, words, and sentences are arranged on the page, but also for the design and emotional qualities of the letterforms themselves. Good typography is a true sign of a talented designer, so it is important to make sure typeface choices are appropriate and their implementation is flawless.

Typefaces have unique characteristics and expressive qualities that allow the designer to identify and properly specify a font for use in a page layout. Composed of many different parts, the anatomy of a typeface is rather complex. The attentive designer places a priority on selecting the right typeface for the visual solution, one that will help communicate the intended message. Some considerations for the selection of a font include the physical form a printed piece will take and the type of paper it will be printed on. For example, in book design, Garamond or Caslon may be used for their well-proportioned letter widths and clean serifs, which make reading easier. Newspapers use Times New Roman or similar serif typefaces with large x-heights and open counter forms so that when printed on coarse newsprint, the ink spread ("dot gain") doesn't fill in the negative space of certain letters.

By choosing typefaces that are similar to or coordinate with those used in existing client collateral, the designer can help establish a more cohesive, consistent brand image. To find suitable matches, study the subtle nuances of certain letters of the typeface. For example, the letters "y," "Q," "g," and the ampersand all yield valuable clues to specifying an appropriate or nearly identical typeface.

Type Considerations

Serifs vs. Sans Serifs

Serif typefaces are considered to be friendly, approachable, and easier to read when used for large amounts of text. Sans serifs are very clean, modern, and "corporate" looking. Create contrast within a design or layout by mixing the use of serif and sans serif fonts.

Italics

Italic letters or words add emphasis to text. Right leaning italics suggest forward movement in Western culture, while left leaning italics convey the idea of slowing down. In cultures that read from right to left, the opposite is true.

Justification

Text that lines up to the left side of a column with varying lengths to the right is generally considered easier to read for left-to-right reading languages ("aligned left, ragged right"). In cultures that read from right to left, the opposite is true.

Center justified text is aligned on both sides of a column and has equal line widths. Long passages of justified text can be difficult to read because there are sometimes large gaps between words, creating "rivers" of white space that interrupt the flow of text. Justified text should only be used for short pieces of copy.

Rag

The edge of a column of text is where lines of copy end. A "clean" rag occurs in lines of copy when there is a nice flow and transition of text from one line to the next and in which there are no hyphenated words at the end of a line. This is the most desirable format, and often requires manipulation on the part of the designer.

Hyphenation

If at all possible, hyphenated text should be avoided, especially in narrow columns. If a word must be hyphenated to create a clean rag, that is acceptable. Never have consecutive lines of hyphenated text.

Kerning

The amount of space between each letter within a word is called kerning. When letters are too close together, they become difficult to read, especially from far away. Likewise, letters spaced far apart are easier to read from afar, yet more difficult to read from up close.

Leading

The term "leading" comes from letterpress printing when actual pieces of lead of varying widths were placed between each line of set type. In the digital world, this term still refers to the amount of space between each line of text. In narrow columns, too much leading tends to make text disconnected. In wider columns, too little leading can fatigue the eyes, making text difficult to read. While there is no mathematical formula that dictates the appropriate amount of leading that should be used in a block of copy, leading looks best when it is at least 3 or 4 points greater than the type size; for example, 12-point-type with 15-point or 16-point leading will have optimum line spacing.

Column Width

For ideal line width and readability, there should only be approximately 12 words per line (50 to 60 characters) within a column of text, otherwise eye fatigue may result.

Widows and Orphans

Widows are lines of text containing only one word. To help alleviate this problem, simply adjust the kerning of a paragraph. Orphans occur when one to two lines of text have jumped to the next column. Both of these scenarios should be avoided.

Hanging Punctuation

When using pull quotes, "hanging" quotation marks to the left of the copy block optically aligns the text.

The anatomy of a typeface is filled with subtle nuances and characteristics that when viewed with a discerning eye can be a powerful tool within the designer's toolbox. Carefully examining the key features of a font is useful in determining the appropriate typeface for a project or for matching a client's current collateral.

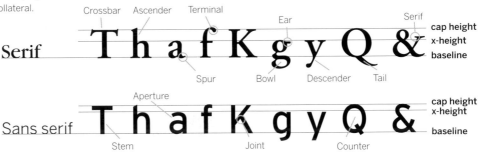

Serif

Crossbar Ascender Terminal Ear Serif cap height x-height baseline

Spur Bowl Descender Tail

Sans serif

Aperture cap height x-height baseline

Stem Joint Counter

Align Left, ragged right text block

When setting large areas of text, it is best to use text that is ragged right, aligned left. This will create the optimum readibility for the viewer of the piece. Line lengths should be no more than 50 characters. Hyphenation should be avoided, and always have the appropriate amount of leading between sentences.

Rivers, widows and hyphenation

When setting large areas of text, it is best to use text that is ragged right, aligned left. This will create the optimum readibility for the viewer of the piece. Line lengths should be no more than 50 characters. Hyphenation should be avoided, and always have the appropriate amount of leading between sentences.

Leading too loose

When setting large areas of text, it is best

to use text that is ragged right, aligned left.

This will create the optimum readibility

for the viewer of the piece. Line lengths

should be no more than 50 characters.

Hyphenation should be avoided, and

always have the appropriate amount of

leading between sentences.

Leading too tight

When setting large areas of text, it is best to use text that is ragged right, aligned left. This will create the optimum readibility for the viewer of the piece. Line lengths should be no more than 50 characters. Hyphenation should be avoided, and always have the appropriate amount of leading between sentences.

When setting large blocks of text in a composition, the designer should use column widths and leading in proportion to the size of type used. Rivers, the gaps of space between words that span several lines of copy, are best avoided by using left justified, ragged right formatting, which is also easier to read.

The image on this cover is arresting, powerful, and evokes feelings of confinement, rebellion, and consequences. Tied conceptually to the content of a feature article, photography adds an extra level of depth and meaning to the visual solution.
Design: Eason & Associates

Imagery

Photography

Photography has the ability to capture the essence of the world around us by freezing moments in time. Photography is a powerful medium that, when used properly in page layout and design, can have enormous impact on the reader—it attracts the viewers' attention and entices them to explore the rest of a printed piece. To achieve this goal, however, photography must be unique and visually appealing, with a distinct focal point. Short depth of field, tight cropping, and close-ups of the subject matter are all ways to accomplish this goal.

Finding the right imagery for a layout is sometimes a challenging task. Sometimes the client will provide the designer with "snapshot" images usually taken with a point-and-shoot or digital camera.

Unique crops, vivid color imagery, and an angular composition attract viewers to this ad promoting the 75th anniversary of a stocking and legging company. Incorporating the flowing robe into the shape of text helps highlight the text of the piece.
Design: Ideo

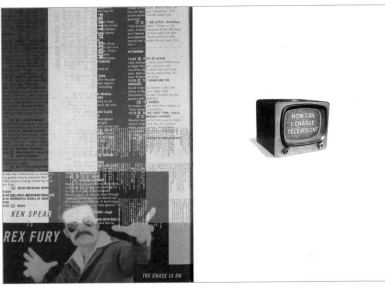

Imagery is a key component of the design for this brochure for Zeum. The cover resembles the back of a painting, forcing the audience to do a double take when viewing the piece for the first time. The captivating images and handwritten text on interior spreads move people through the document.
Design: Cahan & Associates

The message behind this Sesame Workshop annual report is that the organization strives to highlight the international and ethnic diversity of its programming. To convey this, "Hello Friend" is written throughout the opening pages in various languages over images of country-specific Sesame Street characters. A silver metallic varnish of all the different translations for "hello" is printed over each spread to continue the theme.
Design: SamataMason

Typically, the quality of such images suffers due to low resolution, a lack of lighting, experience, or knowledge of compositional techniques. If one of these scenarios should occur, the designer has the option to explore the use of stock photography or to hire a professional photographer.

Commissioned Photography

Depending upon the client's budget and needs, commissioned photography can provide custom imagery for page layout solutions. Traditional commissioned photography is usually shot on location or in a studio, and is art-directed so the exact image the designer envisions is captured. Bracketed exposures allow different angles and lighting techniques to be used, all in an attempt to find an image that is the perfect fit for the project's concept. Because of the extra time involved and the complexity of setting up such an exact, staged photograph, commissioned photography may be cost-prohibitive for some clients.

Depending on the type of image desired, or the reproduction requirements of a particular piece (such as final size of the image or the type of printing process that will be used), the photographer may choose to shoot images using a high-resolution digital camera or a 35mm film camera. A variety of single-lens reflex (SLR) film and digital cameras are available today, all with comparable image quality. The biggest difference between digital and 35mm photography is time and money. Film negatives must be processed, printed, and then scanned into the computer for manipulation. Digital cameras capture data electronically and save it into a computer file, which saves both cost and time. Because of this, most commercial photographers are switching to digital format, but some and are still holding out because they feel the quality is still not as good as with film. Regardless of which format is used, excellent quality can be achieved with both.

The following are examples of websites where stock photography and illustration may be found. Simply registering with the site allows the designer to download low-resolution comp images for use in client presentations and mock-ups.

ACEstock (UK)	www.ace.captureweb.co.uk
Action Press (Germany)	www.actionpress.de
AGE Fotostock (Spain)	www.agefotostock.com
alt.type (Singapore)	www.alttype.biz
Amana Images (Japan)	www.amana.jp
Apeiron Photos (Greece)	www.apeironphotos.com
ArabianEye (U.A.E.)	www.arabianeye.com
Aura Photo Agency (Italy)	www.auraphoto.it
Bildmaschine (Germany)	www.bildmaschine.de
Contrast (Czech Republic)	www.contrast.cz
Corbis (United States)	www.corbis.com
Epictura (France)	www.epictura.com
Fotosearch (United States)	www.fotosearch.com
Getty Images (United States)	www.gettyimages.com
Granata Press Service (Italy)	www.granatapress.com
Hollandse Hoogte (Holland)	foto.hollandse-hoogte.nl
Images.com (United States)	www.images.com
Imagepoint (Switzerland)	www.imagepoint.biz
iStockphoto (United States)	www.istockphoto.com
Photonica (United States)	www.photonica.com
Sambaphoto (Brazil)	www.sambaphoto.com
Sinopix (Hong Kong)	sinopix.com
Stockbyte (United Kingdom)	www.stockbyte.com
Veer (United States)	www.veer.com

Stock Photography

Today there is a plethora of quality "stock" photography available for use in page layout and design. While traditional commissioned photography may be impractical for use in a visual solution due to complexities such as special locations or the cost of hiring models, stock photography is abundant and easy to purchase and download from the Web. Searchable by keyword, numerous websites that contain tens of thousands of photographs on almost any topic or subject matter provide an invaluable resource and reference for designers.

This brochure for ScanChan (Scandinavian Channel) uses an accordion fold, bright colors, and minimal amounts of copy to deliver the brand message that it caters to people of all nationalities. On the reverse, the viewer is greeted with life-size faces of people from a variety of countries.
Design: SamataMason

There are two types of stock photography: royalty-free images, which, once purchased, can be used for multiple layouts or projects without further payment; and rights-managed photography, which incurs recurring licensing fees. Typically, rights-managed images are higher quality and have limited availability and a set period of time in which they may be used. This prevents two companies within similar industries from using an identical image in marketing collateral. Although the quality and originality of images continues to develop, stock photography is not without its drawbacks. As the use of stock images becomes increasingly popular with designers and clients, the price for their use is also increasing—and because they are not specific to any one company or client, they can have a "generic" look. That being said, the work varies greatly from agency to agency, some extremely generic and some quite unique, so shop around.

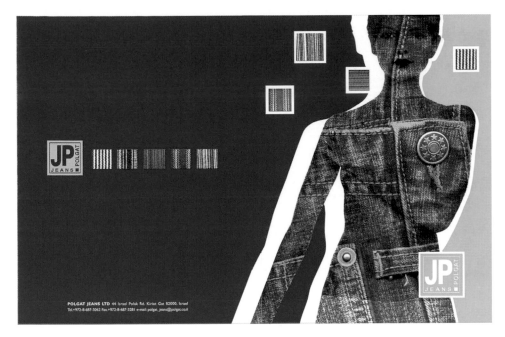

The designer's use of a silhouetted woman filled with a detail of denim jeans creates an intriguing image for this pocket folder promoting Polgat Jeans.
Design: Shira Shechter Studio

Using Found Images

Designers must always obtain permission to use or buy licensing rights for stock photography or other types of imagery within a design project. It is both unethical and illegal to steal someone else's work, and using an image without permission constitutes copyright infringement. While the laws protecting original works of art and design (including photography and illustration) vary from country to country, there are some uses that fall under what is deemed "fair use."

In the United States, students of design may use copyrighted images and illustrations within their work for educational purposes as long as the original artist or designer is credited with the work and the design solution will not be reproduced, distributed, or sold. Images that come from the United States Federal Government are considered to be within the public domain and therefore are free to use (i.e., pictures taken from space that appear on NASA's website fall within this category). Additionally, images that are printed in old magazines or advertisements may also be within the public domain since copyright laws afford only limited protection of a work. Check with your local copyright office to determine if the images you wish to use are still regulated under copyright or if they are in the public domain. For current legal issues affecting found images, contact your local government or an intellectual property attorney.

In order to effectively communicate a message, the designer must use appropriate images and copy that resonates with the target audience. A film aficionado can relate to the annoying arrogance of certain film critics, making the humor of this piece relevant to the audience.
Design: Bradley & Montgomery

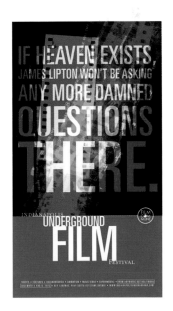

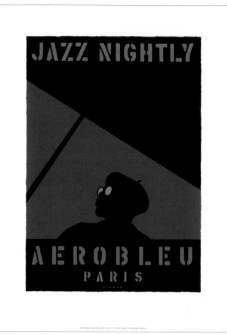

The Complete Graphic Designer

Illustration

Like photography, illustration draws a viewer into the printed page and helps reinforce the message that is being communicated. In addition to the technical and compositional techniques employed by photography, illustration has unique stylistic qualities that may vary depending on concept and execution. For example, the media used to create an illustration establishes a tone or mood for the piece; pastels project light, airy, and even whimsical qualities, while bolder graphics with defined or harsh outlines can put viewers on edge. Cartoon-like caricatures often have comical attributes, while realistic paintings and illustrations convey warmth and familiarity.

Regardless of how an illustration is rendered, it is important that the designer carefully consider how it contributes to the overall effectiveness of a layout. Illustration can be more effective at communicating an idea or a feeling than photography and is sometimes more appropriate when a subject is difficult or painful. Some clients, such as domestic violence shelters or agencies that help children, are not able to use photos due to privacy concerns and so must rely on created imagery.

An illustrated mural adorns the wall at Tatti Café, an Israeli coffee and wine bar. The illustration uses colors and stylistic conventions consistent with the café's identity, and shows happy customers socializing with one another while enjoying their coffee and wine.
Design: Shira Shechter Studio

This poster promotes the use of both sides of business paper in order to conserve natural resources and costs. The two-faced man is perceived first, followed by the headline. Upon closer examination of the work, the viewer discovers that the background actually contains the body copy, facts about recycling.
Design: Dotzero Design

The Complete Graphic Designer

Using a tabloid newspaper layout for the promotion of the play, *Bat Boy*, there is a clear hierarchy of elements on the page. A dominant visual and headline demand attention, the date of the show is secondary, followed by smaller blocks of text, and then finally the body copy.
Design: Archrival

When using illustration in page layout and design, the versatile graphic designer may also act as the illustrator for the piece. However, if time is of the essence or if the project requires a highly stylized or complex illustration, a professional illustrator or stock illustration may be a better option.

As is the case with stock photography, there are advantages and disadvantages to using stock illustration. It is relatively inexpensive and easy to purchase and download from websites. It can be difficult, however, to find the exact image that will work with a particular concept. In this case, select an illustration style that will fit the needs of the project (by searching stock sites or stock illustration books) and then contact the illustrator about creating a custom piece. Illustrators are great conceptual thinkers and will often work with the designer to develop an appropriate and original solution to the problem.

Some ways of creating dynamic compositions that use visual hierarchy are:

1. Size: Larger elements appear to be in the foreground and closer to the viewer; smaller objects appear to be in the background of a piece and therefore appear less prominent or important.

2. Shape: Unique shapes within a layout draw attention. If square or rectangular copy blocks are used, incorporating a circular element or a free-form shape will break the monotony of the piece and draw the viewer's eye to that object.

3. Color: Warm colors such as red or yellow will pop off the page and look as though they are in the foreground. Cooler colors appear to recede into the background.

4. Contrast: Creating contrast between two or more elements draws attention to them. Large shapes or text placed next to smaller elements create a dynamic relationship that pulls those objects closer to the viewer.

5. Movement: Creating a logical sequence or order within a layout guides the viewer's eyes from one element to the next and creates a strong visual hierarchy. Arrows, rules, or Gestalt principles such as similarity or proximity may also achieve this goal. Avoid leading a viewer's eye off of the page to keep them engaged with the piece.

Visual Hierarchy

Once the designer has garnered the attention of the viewer and drawn them into a page layout, it is important that they remain engaged in the piece. By determining the order in which page elements are best perceived, the designer can guide the viewer's eyes around the layout from the most important to the least important pieces of information. This promotes effective communication and comprehension by the viewer.

Compositionally, visual hierarchy is achieved by contrasting elements on a page. Contrast in size, shape, and color determine the order in which the reader perceives and then digests the visual information. If all elements are the same size or similar in color, there will be no logical progression for the viewer to follow, which may result in confusion or frustration. Typically, the largest item on a page or spread will be the first to be read, but this is not always the case—a small red dot on a dark background can be just as effective at catching the attention of the viewer. The hierarchy of the page should logically present the information.

A giant gift resembles the front of a cruise ship in this poster promoting a toy drive for cruise line employees.
Design: Greteman Group

TOYS AHOY
ANNUAL HOLIDAY TOY DRIVE
NOV 24 thru DEC 12

This ad campaign effectively communicates the product and its attributes even though very few elements appear on the page. Instead of lengthy copy or headlines, it relies on visual metaphors to compare the Sparks energy drink with batteries that power and boost performance.
Design: Turner Duckworth

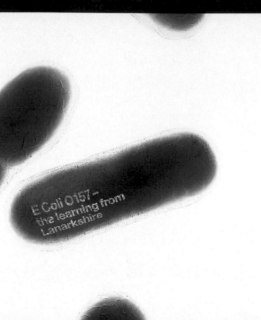

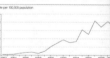

Clean layouts and clear organization of content allow readers of this Department of Health Annual Report learn more about the state of health in England. Cyan-colored text highlights key

> " Even though it requires no extensive schooling, design is one of the most perplexing pursuits in which to excel. Besides the need for God-given talent, the designer must contend with encyclopedic amounts of information, a seemingly endless stream of opinions, and the day-to-day problem of finding 'new' ideas (popularly called creativity)."
>
> —Paul Rand, *Design Form and Chaos*

Chapter 4: **Common**

Design Jobs

In order to successfully craft effective designs, the complete graphic designer must possess the talent, resourcefulness, and flexibility needed to continually respond to the ever-changing needs of his client and industry. With each new technological advance or method of distributing information comes the unique challenge of using those innovations to their best advantage.

Client Considerations

Clients depend on the designer to help solve their marketing and communication problems and send effective visual messages; designers depend on paying clients to make a living, pay expenses, and fulfill their desire to create. The relationship between the two should be one of mutual respect, common goals, and the ability to learn from one another. Realistic expectations in terms of cost and deliverables need to be established up front in any designer/client relationship.

While working for a paying client, the designer is typically not given free reign or complete creative control to develop an artistic masterpiece. Sometimes aesthetic compromises on the designer's part must be made to fulfill a communicative function. One way to exercise full creative control is to work with "not

This brochure for Virgin Airlines uses a chipboard book with a die-cut window to send an effective and clear message to potential customers. The use of extremely simple symbols and phrases ensures the audience will take the moment to flip through it and connect with the brand. By focusing on alleviating the common stresses passengers experience and emphasizing their attention to taking care of the details, Virgin is able to speak to customers' most common needs.
Design: Turner Duckworth

This poster for the Penrod Arts Fair uses intricate typography, layered imagery, and brush strokes suggestive of a painted canvas. An artist palette is inferred through the use of negative shapes, and the circular pattern of color swatches completing the "O" makes its messaging immediate and effective.
Design: Lodge Design

for profit" or "pro bono" clients such as the ballet, symphony, food kitchens, and shelters. They usually have very little or no marketing or advertising budget, yet require effective design to raise money for their causes. In these instances, the designer contributes time and talent at a reduced rate or free of charge (pro bono) to design pieces that promote the organization or its services.

Design for not-for-profits is a noble cause that should be approached cautiously. While many of these clients offer "creative freedom" as a perk, there is often a committee that must sign off and approve the work, each member of which has his own agenda and opinion. Additionally, once committed to working with a nonprofit client, the designer is often repeatedly asked to donate his or her services to the cause. Because of these issues, it is sometimes more beneficial for the graphic designer to relinquish some creative freedom and receive full compensation for his services.

This ad for Pick Up uses a large illustration combined with product photography in the background to effectively showcase the company's selection of bar stools and chairs.
Design: Shira Shechter Studio

Advertisements that require user interaction are highly effective marketing tools. Die cut holes on this flyer invite potential customers to "try out" a new Nokia game phone.
Design: Kinetic

The Complete Graphic Designer

Advertisements

Advertisements are page layout design problems that promote a product, company or its services. Creating an effective solution that quickly communicates the who, what, when, where, why, and how of an advertiser's message represents a unique challenge for the graphic designer. Strong visuals must be incorporated to draw viewers into the composition, while well-written headlines reinforce the visuals and entice them to read further. Most importantly, effective advertisements should establish a clear hierarchy of information.

Always be sure to contact the publication in which the ad will appear to confirm the dimensions of the ad and by what means it will be reproduced. Advertising space varies in size from fractional pages (such as one-quarter, one-half or one-third page) to a full-page spread, sometimes spanning multiple pages or spreads. Designing newspaper ads can be more of a challenge for the designer in that they are usually specified in "column inches," which allows for flexible sizes depending on the publication. To determine the exact dimensions for one of these ads, divide the column inches by the number of columns wide to determine the height of the ad—for example, a 36 column-inch ad may be 12" tall and 3 columns wide or 9" tall and 4 columns wide.

Showing cans of Sparks energy drink as a replacement for the batteries of a powered subwoofer suggests that the beverage boosts performance to maximum levels.
Design: Turner Duckworth

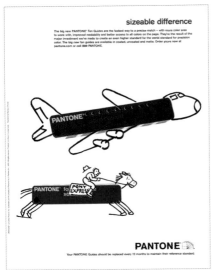

To promote the larger size of the new Pantone® swatch books, these pared down, eye-catching ads use whimsical illustrations to communicate the difference between the old, smaller version by comparing a skyscraper with a house, a giraffe with a camel, and an airplane with a horse.
Design: And Partners

Components of Effective Advertising Layout:

1. Strong visual or graphics

Arresting photography or illustration makes the ad stand out from surrounding competitors. Likewise, a lot of white space can have the same effect, depending on the surrounding material.

2. Headline

Appealing to the audience's emotions or intellect with a well-crafted and conceptual headline will make for a more effective advertisement.

3. Body copy

Supporting copy should be concise and to the point, and a clear hierarchy of information must be presented to the viewer.

4. Call to Action

What do you want the viewer to do—make a phone call? Visit a website? To inspire a reader to action, it is important to first entice viewer interaction with a piece.

5. Contact information

No matter how clever or well designed, if an ad does not give the viewer a way to contact the company for more information, it will fail to attract new customers.

6. Logo

The client logo should always appear on sales promotions or ads, as they identify a company or organization and establish consistency in visual communications.

7. Violators

Starbursts, turned-page graphics, and bold, garish colors are all effective ways to call attention to a piece of information. These are called "violators" because they typically do not resemble any other element on the page. These must be used with caution, as they are not appropriate for every ad. For example, they can disrupt an elegant solution, so use them wisely.

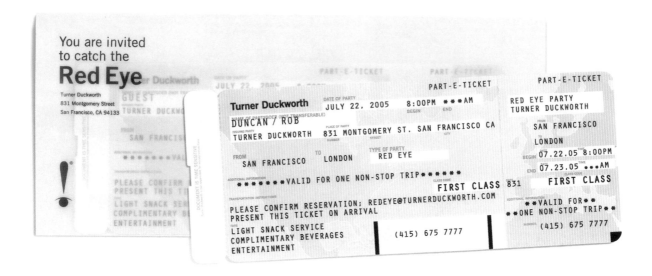

Playing off the idea of a "red eye" flight, Turner Duckworth's Red Eye Party invitation resembles a boarding pass. A translucent envelope reveals the unique format of the piece, persuading recipients to open it.
Design: Turner Duckworth

Printed Collateral

The creation of sales and marketing collateral for a client is one of the most common jobs a graphic designer is commissioned to do. That being said, they are by no means easy to design or produce, as specifications for collateral vary from job to job depending on the client, target audience, and the function of the piece. The one constant, however, is that the concept behind the design must always drive the piece and meet the ultimate goals for the project, such as introducing a new brand image or showcasing a company's products or services.

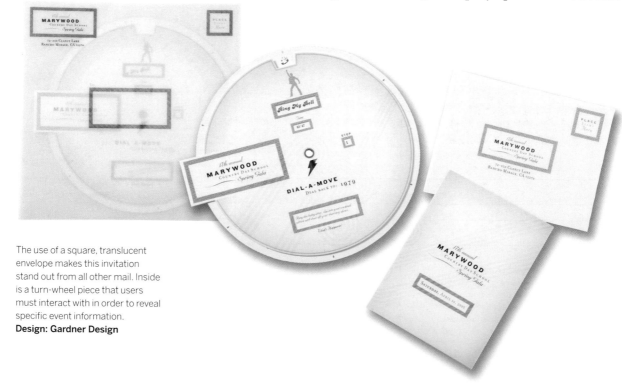

The use of a square, translucent envelope makes this invitation stand out from all other mail. Inside is a turn-wheel piece that users must interact with in order to reveal specific event information.
Design: Gardner Design

Invitations and announcements are not just single pieces; they consist of several components that work together as part of the design. Keep these considerations in mind when presenting design options to a client:

- Pertinent information about an event must be prominently featured on the invitation.
- Provide specific details such as location, date, time, and purpose in a clear and easy-to-find location.
- Carefully consider which elements are important to include.
- In addition to the piece itself, a reply card and envelope, a map and directions to the event, other information sheets may be necessary. These should all fit into one large, outer envelope.
- Confirm postage for any oddly shaped or sized pieces. Pieces that fall outside of the proportions established by the U.S. Postal Service require additional postage to mail. Always confirm the rate for any uniquely shaped or sized pieces with the post office, as well as your client, so there are no surprises.
- Whenever possible, provide postage for reply cards.
- Using pre-paid or stamped reply envelopes will increase the chances that people will respond to an invitation.

Invitation Design

When designing invitations and announcements, it is essential to make eye-catching exteriors that do not blend in with other mail or get mistaken for junk mail. Specialty paper, unique shapes, or stylistic conventions that require audience participation ensure a design solution will be opened. The exterior also provides an opportunity to establish a mood or tone through the use of typography and visuals. Because invitations are usually not complex pieces with large amounts of information, they are fairly open to interpretation. They can be as subdued and elegant as a traditionally engraved wedding invitation, or as wild as the imagination can conjure. Many incorporate objects that reflect the theme of the event and push the boundaries by printing on unusual surfaces. As with every job, it all depends on the client and their budget, but it is important to discuss the breadth of options so the end result will be as compelling as it can be. A dynamic invitation will always yield a larger crowd.

This kit for the opening of a children's art center invites the recipient to use his imagination to "create art" by sculpting a large block of clay. The simple typographic treatment uses selected red letters within the word "create" to effectively communicate the purpose of the piece.
Design: Cahan & Associates

A series of three posters advertises the National Rock Paper Scissors Collegiate Championship through bold graphics and bright colors. When viewed individually, the hand gestures have dual meaning. The rock sign also means "power," the scissor sign "peace," and the paper sign "stop."
Design: Archrival

Posters

The first goal of every poster is to grab the attention of passersby and immediately communicate the intended message. With our world becoming increasingly cluttered with lights, signs, billboards, and flyers, creating dynamic posters that stand out among the visual noise and connect with viewers is increasingly difficult. Because of this, a strong visual concept that requires little if any text to communicate and a clear hierarchy are paramount.

Because these posters were placed in urban environments on concrete posts or brick walls, the designer chose bold, bright colors to attract attention and coarse illustrations with visible halftone patterns to reinforce their urban appeal.
Design: Archrival

Posters have the power to communicate with very few words. In this bold yet simple design, the headline plays off of the winery name, Gloria Ferrer.
Design: Michael Schwab Studio

Poster Design Considerations

Physical location

When designing a poster, take into consideration where the poster will be hung. Will it be inside a building, well-lit, among numerous other posters on a busy thoroughfare, or will it be folded and sent in the mail? Determine if your viewers will have time to stop and observe the poster, in which case you can afford to create a more intricate work; or if you need to catch their eyes and communicate the message in a few seconds with a bold and simplistic composition. Every scenario will require a different design strategy for success.

Size

Large posters are more effective at grabbing viewer attention. The only restrictions are where the poster will be displayed, the size of the printing press, and the client's budget.

Color

Posters utilizing bright, vibrant colors tend to pop off a surface unless they are hung in a sea of equally vibrant works. In this case, a one- or two-color piece can be just as, if not more, effective.

Typography

In a world where viewers are over-stimulated by graphic images and messages, a poster utilizing simple typography will stand out and convey its information most efficiently. Depending on the characteristics of a selected font, typography has the ability to convey emotional and expressive qualities. Sans serif fonts are very direct and authoritative looking, while serif and italic types are friendlier and more approachable.

Imagery

Simple and direct visuals attract the viewer's attention and compel them to read presented information. Generally speaking, images should dominate the composition unless a typographic solution is used.

A photomontage of imagery, color, and textures combine to advertise the Palace of Fine Arts in San Francisco. The poster's narrow format gives the work and subject a commanding feel, while the painterly qualities convey the venue's approachability.
Design: Michael Cronan Design

The Complete Graphic Designer

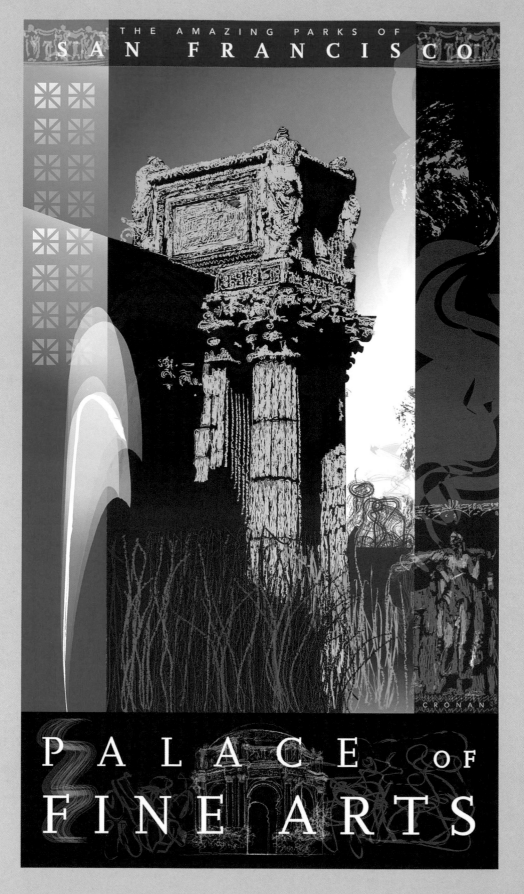

The secret to creating a great brochure is to entice the viewer to open the cover. In this brochure, the simple graphic of a tie on the front prompts reader curiosity. As the viewer is drawn in further, dramatic imagery and bold typography keeps the reader engaged. Avoiding large amounts of copy ensures that the piece will be read.
Design:
Hornall Anderson Design Works

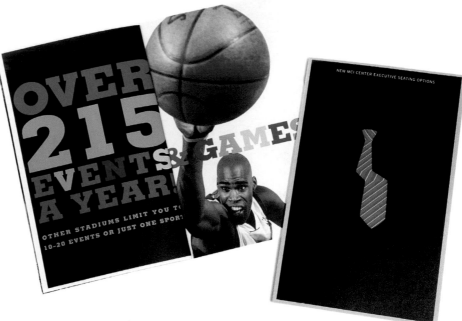

Brochure Design

A brochure's goal is to present a company, its products, or services in a unique and interesting way that not only grabs the viewer's attention, but prompts them to contact the company. The combination of strong visual images with clearly written and concise messages makes for the best design solution.

A brochure should answer the following questions in a succinct and easy-to-follow format: What does the company do? How can the reader get more information? And most importantly, how will the reader benefit from their product or services? Creating a strong written message is imperative, and there are two ways to ensure the content meets the needs of the piece—the designer can work with the client to develop the content, or the client or designer can hire a professional copywriter.

To convince potential customers about their client's knowledge of building materials, the designers created a dimensional brochure for Tin Tab. Dimensional pieces often garner more attention than traditional folded ones.
Design: Aloof Design

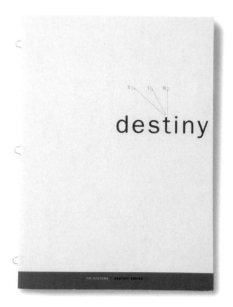

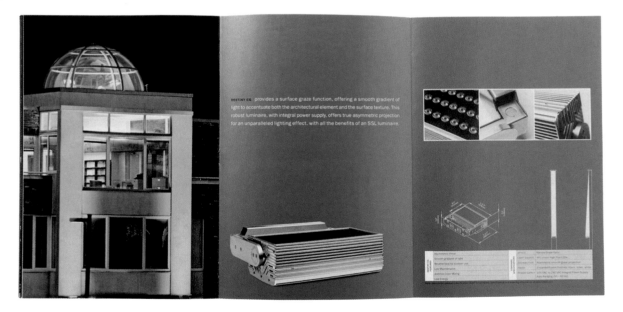

For a brand of colorful outdoor lights, this sales piece utilizes metallic silver printing throughout to contrast with the vivid color photography that shows products in action. Fold-out flaps for each style of light show product specifications through the use of line art diagrams and charts, while a loop-stitch binding allows the brochure to be stored in a three-ring binder.
Design: SamataMason

Brochures do not have to be four-color to enhance a client's image. Bluestem Restaurant achieved a high-end, elegant look by combining artistic, black-and-white photography with a sophisticated layout. A tightly cropped duotone image of grass makes for a dramatic and thought-provoking cover.
Design: Indicia Design

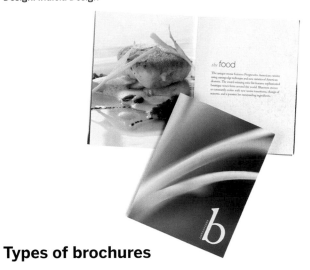

- Entice the reader to open the brochure and read more about a company, product, or service. The designer has approximately six seconds to grab the viewer's attention.

- Establish awareness about a company, organization, or product through interesting visuals and well-developed copy.

- Provide useful and relevant information so the viewer will want to keep the brochure for future reference.

- Direct readers to seek out more information through the use of a "Call to Action." This can include a phone number, email address, or website.

Types of brochures

1. Capability
Focuses on communicating the services a company provides

2. Sales/Marketing
Presents detailed information about specific products including features and pricing information

3. Image
Introduces a new brand or corporate image

4. Informational
Presents pertinent information about a specific topic or issue the audience is interested in and provides a way for them to get more information by directing them to a website or phone number

To educate and inform on the safety and use of original Nokia batteries and accessories, an instructional card with a hangtag was shipped in a translucent silver mailer. A simple wrap-around label was used for addressee information, which did not distract the viewer from the most important pieces inside.
Design: Yellow Octopus

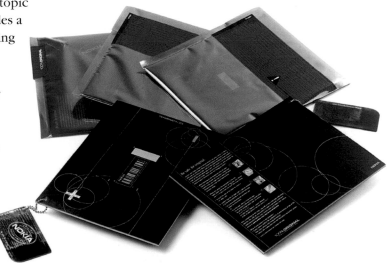

Bold color and illustration styles appeal to children. This piece merges the function of a foundation's annual report with an actual children's book. Whimsical illustration visually interprets the story, while facts for adults and information about contributors appear at the bottom of the page.
Design: Greteman Group

Publication Design

A publication's primary functions are to entertain, educate, or present reference material in a logical and easy-to-use format. Therefore, it is essential that the design does not inhibit the reader's comprehension of the material. Although some publications stray from basic rules of typography and layout, it is best to follow traditional design conventions unless the client requests otherwise.

Clean and consistent layouts with a logical flow from page to page can be achieved through the use of a well-structured grid. By devising visual systems for specific types of information such as captions, chapter openers, and sidebars, readers will be able to navigate the piece with ease. It is also important to remember that large amounts of text tend to fatigue the eyes; therefore ample "white" or negative space, proportional column width, and appropriate leading for the type size are important things to keep in mind.

All publications, from novels and annual reports to user manuals and magazines, have a different audience and a different function, so each requires a unique design solution. Depending on the amount of information and the target audience, the designer must create a format that will engage the audience and deliver content in an appropriate and well thought-out manner.

Architectural and graphic standard guides for federal buildings are compartmentalized into separate volumes. A slipcase allows all pieces to be stored in the same place for easy reference and portability.
Design: C&G Partners

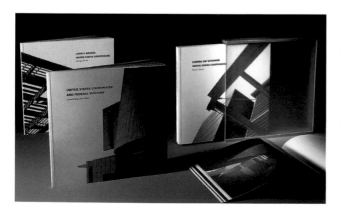

A large masthead (logo) dominates the front of How Magazine, demanding viewer attention when displayed on magazine racks. The use of illustration instead of traditional photography for the cover also helps establish shelf presence for the publication.
Design: Pentagram

Publication Design Considerations

Type size should be appropriate for the audience. For a general audience, font sizes should be no less than 9 points in large bodies of text, but elderly people tend to have weaker eyesight and require 12- or 13-point text. Children that are learning to read also require large print to help them decipher individual letters and sounds.

Books or publications must be easily navigable. To help readers find and comprehend the information they need, use sections or chapters to organize content. A complete table of contents and an index for complex works will clarify the structure and increase the overall effectiveness of the piece. Never underestimate the value of folios (page numbers). They are essential and should be easy to locate on the page.

Shelf presence

Dust jackets and covers not only provide protection for a book, they advertise the content. Most of the time, only the spines of books are visible. Incorporating vibrant color or graphics helps the piece stand out from others on a bookstore or library shelf. Make sure the name of the piece is clearly legible and readable from a distance.

The title for *Rules of the Red Rubber Ball* does not appear on the cover. Instead, a circular swatch of red rubber (the same used to make playground balls) has been inlaid in the chipboard cover above an embossed dotted line. The simple tactile embellishments are enough to entice and engage viewers.
Design: Willoughby Design

Designed with the audience in mind, these books appeal to graphic designers—smaller type sizes are used in each of these solutions because a clean layout and minimal text is preferred. Simplified illustrations with large blocks of color reinforce the content, while a solid grid structure defines an easy-to-follow visual hierarchy.
Design: Shinnoske, Inc.
Below: Willoughby Design

Binding Techniques

Depending on the amount of text and the width of a final publication, the designer will need to decide what type of binding to use. Some options are as follows:

Case Binding

A durable but expensive solution for longer publications

Perfect Binding

A moderately durable choice for longer publications that is less expensive than case binding

Saddle Stitch

A fast and low-cost solution for shorter publications such as magazines

Side Stitch

A fast and low-cost solution with a variety of sizing options. More durable that than saddle stitch

Screw and Post

A fast and low-cost solution with the benefit of being able to add or remove pages after binding

Tape

A moderately durable and less-expensive solution than case binding but does not allow for a printed spine

Plastic Comb

A good solution for small runs that do not require high durability. Allows pages to be added and removed after binding

Spiral

A moderately durable and moderately priced solution that can accommodate various types of printed papers or substrates bound into the same publication

Ring

A low-cost option that allows for hand assembly and continual modification of the contents

Clean layouts and clear organization and clear organization of content allow readers of this Department of Health Annual Report to learn more about the state of health in England. Cyan-colored text highlights key points on each spread, while easy-to-read charts and striking photography emphasize the copy.
Design: CDT Design

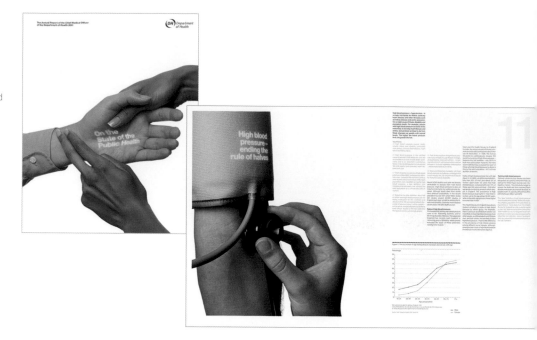

Annual Reports

Every corporation, no matter how large or small, for profit or not-for-profit, is required by law to file an annual report with their state or provincial government—this is especially true of publicly traded national or international companies. These documents, which both profile the company and outline funding and expenditures throughout the fiscal year, provide investors and federal regulators with the ability to review the management's decisions and analyze how the decisions affect the financial health of the organization. Because annual reports contain such a dense concentration of financial information, the portion focused on telling the company's story must work hard at getting the message across clearly and concisely. To get a good sense of how to portray a particular client, research competing companies' reports and review the previous year's report.

Portraying a company in the most positive, professional, and ethical manner possible is the burden the graphic designer carries. Annual reports are the

To promote the idea of growth, the designers chose to feature close-up photography of plants that appear almost as abstract elements and blocks of copy that mimic their shapes for this annual report. To further reinforce this idea, a layer of plastic "grass" has been attached to the front and back covers.
Design: Kinetic

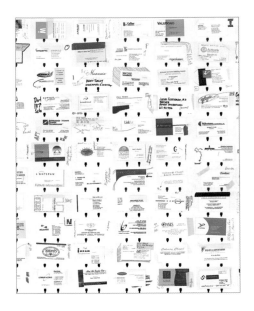

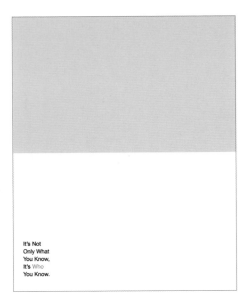

It's Not
Only What
You Know,
It's Who
You Know.

coup de grace of a company's marketing budget, and typically more money and manpower will be spent on these projects than for anything else. Because of this, it is essential to partner with a copywriter or the client's marketing department to ensure that a highly conceptual and appropriate theme or message is developed. The production of the final piece is also important and, for many, only the highest quality printing, paper selections, and attention to detail will suffice. A single typo can cause an entire batch of tens of thousands of books to be thrown out and reprinted, so take extra care when reviewing the final files before they go to press.

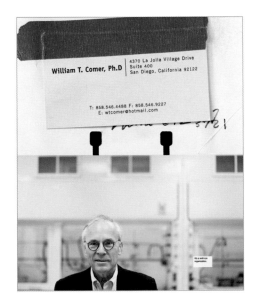

"It's not only what you know, it's who you know," is the message exemplified in this annual report for Silicon Valley Bank. Using Rolodex cards to communicate their theme, the report features success stories about some of the bank's relationships. The use of handwritten text and a casual photographic style adds a personal feel to the report, which further conveys the idea of one-on-one relationships.
Design: Cahan & Associates

Netgear manufactures wireless networking products that are prominently featured in this annual report. In an effort to connect readers to the technology featured, the piece incorporates examples of how specific people use the products at work and at home. The rest of the report relies on thoughtful typography and generous white space to communicate additional information, including a product listing at the back.

Design: Weymouth Design

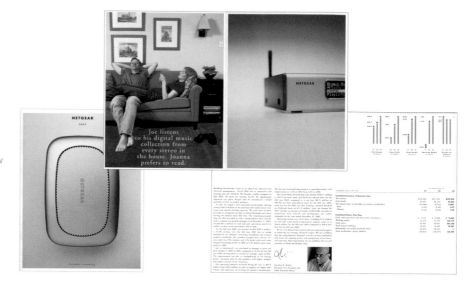

Components of an Annual Report

1. President's Letter
A letter from the company president or chairman informs investors about major events of the previous year and outlines the company's vision and future plans for the organization.

2. Background Information
People review annual reports to learn more about the heritage and tradition of a company. Information about office locations and key personnel (upper management and officers) should be included.

3. Financial Statement
By law, a company's financial statement must be included in an annual report. This statement is usually provided to the designer as an Excel spreadsheet or table detailing a company's revenues, expenses, officer and director compensation, gross and net profits or loss, business assets, and any other data that verifies a company's financial health.

4. Charts and Diagrams
In addition to the year's numbers, visual interpretations of the company's performance in sales (products) or subscribers (services) are presented to current or potential investors of the company. Diagrams such as pie charts should be included for speed and ease of comprehension.

5. Product or Service Offerings
Annual reports should tell potential investors who or what the company is, what it does, and why it matters.

Annual Report Considerations

- Investors respond better to black ink, especially in financial statements. Never use red text in an annual report unless the company experiences a loss in revenue or profits and specifically requests it.

- The most common format is one that divides the report into sections with the company story first followed by the financial statement sections.

- Minimal copy and vivid imagery draw viewers into the piece and make them read more.

- Annual reports are typically perfect bound or saddle stitched. Sometimes they are packaged with other collateral for greater effectiveness.

THAT MEANS MORE STRINGENT AIR QUALITY REGULATIONS ARE BEING ADOPTED IN MORE PARTS OF THE WORLD.

WE LEVERAGE OUR EMISSION-CONTROL EXPERTISE INTO AN EVER-WIDENING RANGE OF MARKETS AND APPLICATIONS.

The rising concern over air quality and how Englehard's technology helps clean and purify the air is the main message of this report. Imagery of children in front of a diesel-burning school bus (traditionally not the cleanest modes of transportation) juxtaposed with a brilliant blue sky that seems fresh and clean appeals to the audience's emotions, while arrows and wide-open layouts reinforce the report's theme.
Design: Addison

NEO
FOR
MA

2002 Annual Report

IN
FOR
M

The Neoforma annual report uses bright spot colors and simple diagrams to illustrate the services the company provides. Ample white space and minimal copy make pages inviting to read.
Design: Cahan & Associates

"Neoforma Market Intelligence from HPIS is the industry standard for accurate, third-party, non-biased data. My team utilizes this data on a daily basis for customer reviews and tracking."

Courier is a leading book publisher that primarily publishes school textbooks. This annual report is designed to look like a primary education schoolbook. A brown paper wrapper, complete with doodles, covers the publication, while various pages have important information highlighted, and financial performance is presented on ruled ledger paper. This whimsical approach combines a unique solution while utilizing the textbook concept to present the information in an easy-to-follow format.

Design: Weymouth Design

Common Design Jobs

In this Pottery Barn Kids catalog, children are shown using the actual products. The use of professional models within a catalog makes the images seem more realistic and the products more appealing.
Design: Cahan & Associates

Catalog Design

Brochures and catalogs have similar functions in that their primary goal is to sell products or services to a specific target market. The difference between them is that brochures tend to feature only one line of products or services, and are used as leave-behind pieces by salespeople who will ultimately follow up with a customer, whereas catalogs contain a variety of items from different product lines, and are delivered to the customer without a sales person to help persuade them into action. The catalog must therefore work harder to engage the viewer through beautiful photography and detailed descriptions.

Catalogs often use imagery that not only appeals to the audience but shows the product in use. North Face, a high-end outdoor apparel company, provides customers with a variety of information by featuring dramatic action and close-up shots that highlight product features and fabrics along with color choices or corresponding accessories.
Design: Satellite Design

The Old House Style Guide for Rejuvenation chose a unique way to showcase its various products. The turn-wheel format allows users to select the decorating period they are interested in and then provides useful background information about that era. Once a style is selected by turning the rotating wheel, appropriate furnishings and fixtures for that time period are displayed through die-cut windows on the back.
Design: Gardner Design

Effective catalogs allow users to quickly locate the information they need. The simplest way to do this is to organize the content into clearly defined and labeled sections that are easy to find and differentiate. These product categories may be defined by the type of item, the function it performs, or where it is used. Graphically, the designer may use large images, headlines, or color coding to indicate the various sections. It is equally imperative that the layout flow from spread to spread is easy to navigate, which a well-defined grid can ensure.

Since buyers usually do not have physical interaction with a product, it is important that featured items are represented accurately in the catalog through clear photography and detailed descriptions. Size, color, price, and other distinguishing characteristics should be highlighted in the body copy for quick recognition.

Common Design Jobs

The clean and contemporary style of West Elm's furniture and accessories are clearly communicated through the geometric layouts of the catalog. Cool colors and a discernable grid lend a clean elegance to the design, while location photography complements the actual products.
Design: Templin Brink

Some catalogs consist of a narrative about a company or its products, or establish a tone for the piece through imagery. Psychedelic patterns adorn the front of this bar stool and chair catalog, while gritty collaged illustrations are interspersed throughout, running alongside the actual product photography.

Design: Shira Shechter Studio

Catalog Design Considerations

1. Contact information

Contact information, including phone numbers and website addresses, is essential to the layout and must appear on every spread in case a customer tears a page from the catalog and would like to place an order.

2. Detailed product photography

Every image should not only show the product in its best light, but the tone of the photography must match the tone of the catalog and convey qualities that express the nature of the brand. Color is critical—what the customer sees in the catalog should clearly reflect the actual item in every way.

3. Navigation

Catalogs should be easy to use. Label all product images with numbers or letters that correspond with descriptions that appear near the photo or in a specific location on the page.

4. Ordering information

Sizing charts, billing information, shipping instructions, and payment details are essential for a successful transaction. Make sure this area is well organized and complete.

This identity for a business consultancy called Katalyst uses the idea of the scientific process. Small icons representing different types of catalysts, such as sunlight, chemicals, and so on appear on the front, while the backs of the cards feature different icons and when put together resemble a Periodic Table of Elements.
Design: Willoughby Design

Translucent envelopes have been effectively used for AgriLite to communicate the idea of how light interacts with plants (the back of the letterhead has an image of a plant leaf and when folded the image shows through the envelope). The designer of this piece carefully considered the placement of the tagline on the back of the sheet so it appears through the envelope in an appropriate location.
Design: Bystrom Design

Chapter 5:

Corporate Identity

Successful corporate identity programs consist of simple, unique, and memorable logos, graphic elements, and color palettes that visually represent the core values, philosophy, and principles of a business. One of the most important attributes of an effective identity campaign is the consistent application of these elements across all forms of company communication, from business cards to on-screen presentations and employee uniforms.

An Identity Is Not a Brand

In recent years, "corporate identity" has been used interchangeably with the term "branding," particularly by overzealous marketing consultants, public relations specialists, and even some creative agencies. The core difference is that an identity is a visual system used to identify a company's goals, values, and personality, while a brand is the impression the market has about a company.

Consistency and Corporate Identity

When undertaking a new corporate identity project, it is imperative for the designer to maintain consistency. Consistency plays a vital role in how a business or organization is perceived by its customers. While ultimately the quality of the products and services of an organization will determine its success, the corporate identity should be a direct reflection of those qualities. If an identity varies greatly from application to application, or selectively appears on marketing collateral, a mixed message is being communicated. This inconsistency can make the audience question the legitimacy of the business.

Where most identities falter in consistency is when transitioning

The Mobil corporate identity program was developed by Chermayeff and Geismar in 1966 with continued consultation and design over thirty-five years. By developing a consistent identity that is incorporated into the design of the company's products, services, and even store architecture, the simple yet unique Mobil logo is now ingrained into the American consumer's psyche as a representation of a leading petroleum company.
Design:
Chermayeff & Geismar Studio

An identity system incorporates all the visual elements with which a customer or client comes into contact. For this Irish restaurant, the identity has been applied to menus, glasses, brochures, and stationery.
Design: Lodge Design

In order to be effective, successful corporate identity programs must consist of the following qualities in all internal and external communications:

- Distinction through unique logos and graphics

- Clarity of message by using consistent graphic elements

- Solidarity, longevity, and memorability

from an older, more established identity to a new one. Instead of using similar color schemes, typefaces, or graphic elements, some organizations try to change their look abruptly, completely disregarding any equity that may have existed in the old identity. This leads to a tumultuous transition and confusion on the part of the customer. Instead of haphazard implementation, a new identity should evolve gradually over time to communicate clarity, solidarity, and distinction.

Corporate identities should be designed for longevity and a minimum life span of five-to-ten years. The most successful identities have remained relatively unchanged for decades, such as ABC (American Broadcasting Company), Westinghouse, United Airlines, and AT&T. Some identities, like AEG (Allgemeine Elektricitats Gesellschaft), London Underground, and GE (General Electric) have been around for more than 100 years.

The multicolored peacock has represented NBC (National Broadcasting Company) since 1956, but wasn't adopted as the official identity until 1985. Since then, it has consistently been shown on-screen during television broadcasts and commercial breaks, representing quality entertainment and news.
Design:
Chermayeff & Geismar Studio

The modern corporate identity stems from the basic human need and desire to communicate individuality, ownership, and origin. As a sign of their nobility, kings and queens had their monograms placed on stately correspondence. In the same vein, heraldry, or the use of family crests and symbols emblazoned on shields, helmets, and dress, was a way for knights and warriors to be identified during competition or battle.

However, this practice of representing oneself with a symbol or mark was not just for the elite. From the ancient Greeks to the middle ages, simple monograms and marks were used as signatures because most people were illiterate. For thousands of years, farmers have branded and labeled livestock with unique symbols to claim them. This long-standing practice also extended to artisans of all types, including potters, stonemasons, glass blowers, and metalworkers, who to this day mark their work with symbols that have become essential in identifying antiquities.

Although corporate identity as we know it today didn't exist until the early twentieth century, and its true potential to identify, differentiate, and influence wasn't realized until the 1950s and 60s, its foundation reaches back to the beginning of civilization.

The best way to increase longevity of an identity is to avoid stylistic trends that will date the mark. During the 1990s, all logos that used a "swoosh" were perceived to be progressive, technologically superior, and geared for growth and expansion. In the early 2000s, as "outsourcing" became a media and marketing buzzword, companies began using globes to convey the idea of global reach or impact on the world economy. Recently, logos have begun appearing more dimensional by incorporating a highlight or sheen, much like a shiny hood ornament on a car. Even veteran companies with long histories and established identities have fallen prey to this new convention: UPS (United Parcel Service) recently adopted a new dimensional badge that lacks much of the simplicity and elegance of Paul Rand's original design from 1960.

Corporate identity communicates a distinct image for a company that must be applied to all forms of visual communication, including printed collateral and apparel. For +CERT.hr, the idea of first aid for computers is communicated through crosses: a cross-shaped brochure, photography of implied crosses on wall posters, and through negative space on t-shirts.
Design: Ideo

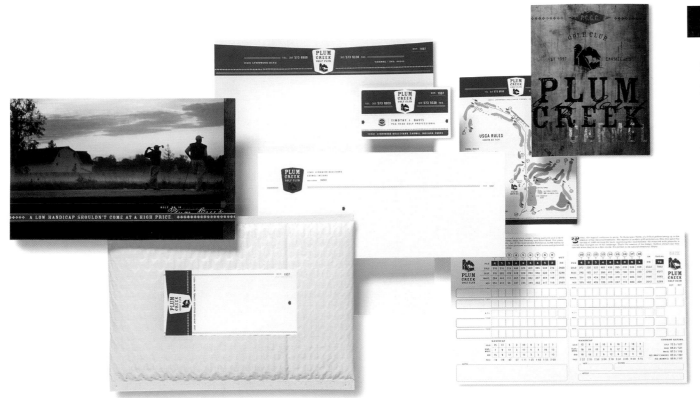

Consistent application of the company's or organization's logo does not mean that the mark has to appear the same way on every piece of collateral. In this identity for a country club, Lodge Design created multiple versions of the logo for use in different applications; the logo may appear in one or two colors and in a variety of formats.
Design: Lodge Design

standard

There is nothing standard about how the identity for Standard is presented. Illustrative icons incorporating the backward "s" are used in various applications and a dynamic palette of colors conveys consistency.
Design: Gardner Design

The Complete Graphic Designer

SPIRIT
AEROSYSTEMS

CitationShares

This logo for Spirit Aerosystems, a company that manufactures components for commercial airplanes, is suggestive of both a star and airplane. Rich blues associated with high-altitude flight have also been incorporated into the color scheme.
Design: Gardner Design

For obvious reasons, blue is a prominent color in aviation and aerospace companies. This logo for CitationShares, an airplane timeshare company, incorporates a deep blue to represent the idea of both the sky and high-altitude flight. Stylized jet windows shown in perspective comprise the logo mark and suggest the idea of a jet taking off.
Design: Hornall Anderson Design Works

Identity Design Considerations

When a larger, mature company undertakes an identity reevaluation, it does so for a variety of reasons. One may be that the focus of the business or scope of services offered has changed. Perhaps the business is expanding through acquisition. Sometimes, when a new CEO or president takes over, they think that change is both inevitable and necessary. Whatever the reason, the first question to ask must be: does the identity need a complete makeover or will a simple enhancement or modernization suffice?

How much change is necessary to revitalize a corporate identity depends on several factors. Psycho-logically, our minds are hardwired to detect and respond to sudden change—when something is suddenly new and different, we immediately recognize the difference and pay attention; conversely, slow and incremental change is much harder to detect. If a company has made big changes, such as in management or the focus of their business, a completely revised mark will call attention to this fact. Sometimes, a company's identity becomes so static and unchanging that it will actually fade in importance in the mind of the customer. For this reason, companies will periodically update their marks by making them more dimensional or changing the typeface.

When GoTo.com's name could no longer be trademarked and its business model changed, C&G Partners was hired to reposition the company and develop a new visual identity. The name Overture was ultimately selected to convey the fact that the company makes introductions to Web content. The two concentric "O"s not only represent the name of the company but also resemble a target.
Design: C&G Partners

Sometimes the designer does not necessarily know how an identity or logo will be used, so it is essential that logos are designed to work at all sizes and for a variety of applications. In this case, the logo for Excalibur knives has been etched into the blade of the knife itself.
Design: Turner Duckworth

Choosing a Style

How a corporate identity will be used is a determining factor for the physical look of the identity. It has been argued that "form follows function" and nowhere is this more true than in the area of corporate identity. The size of the logo, the type of products or collateral it will be placed on, and the amount of time the viewer will have to look at and interact with it are all important things the designer must take into account. Furthermore, it must also appeal to and connect with the emotions and expectations of the target customer or audience. If a logo or identity is not relevant to the intended customer, it will be ineffective and possibly detrimental.

Thoroughly exploring the client's industry and any preconceived ideas and perceptions customers may have toward the company is helpful in determining the type of graphics or motifs that should be used. This initial research will set the design on track from an early stage by establishing a visual vocabulary or point of reference for the new design. If a company has built a tradition through design, the designer must determine the elements that have the most "equity" and build on those strengths. Referencing the old identity reinforces the customer's perception of an organization, and eases the transition from old to new.

Graphic design, especially in the corporate realm, is undertaken to solve unique business problems such as increasing customer recognition, retention, or sales. Corporate identity is a strategic way of solving these needs. A designer's ability to partner with an organization and take a lead role in developing a new corporate identity will cause him to become a trusted consultant and advisor.

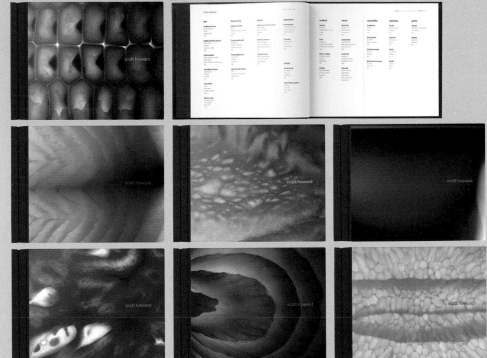

Restaurants, particularly those that are not franchises, require identities that communicate its core values. For Scott Howard, a simple logo is used in conjunction with striking, close-up food photography—so abstracted that they resemble works of art. Brown and orange, two very appetizing colors, are used as the dominant color scheme on everything from menus to check covers.
Design: Turner Duckworth

Corporate Identity

carrot broth
try this at home

5-6 servings
3 cups diced carrots (small dice)
6 1/2 cups carrot juice
Salt & pepper to taste
1 cup heavy cream
1/2 tablespoon curry powder

technique
1. Put diced carrots in a small pot.
2. Cover with carrot juice (reserve remaining for later).
3. Cook carrots in juice until the juice is reduced until dry.
4. In blender, puree cooked carrots (in small batches) with remaining juice until smooth.
5. Return to stove. Slowly heat to a simmer.
6. Add curry powder and then salt and pepper to taste.
7. Add cream
8. Strain through Chinoise (fine mesh strainer).
9. Garnish with cream fraiche and truffle oil.

(415) 956 7040
500 Jackson Street, San Francisco, CA 94133
www.scotthowardsf.com

scott howard

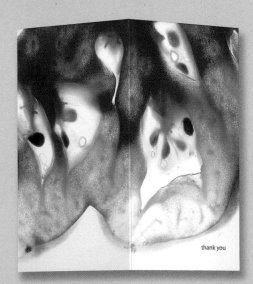

thank you

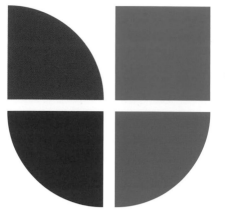

Univision is one of the largest Spanish-language networks and broadcasts to a variety of different markets. The logo is an abstract "U" divided into quadrants with the top left element rotated. The simplicity of the logo and its bold colors makes for an immediately recognizable identity.
Design: Chermayeff & Geismar Studio

DigitalCrowd provides Web hosting and Internet consultation, creating a virtual community of people and businesses, an idea communicated through its graphic but immediately identifiable logo.
Design: Indicia Design

The Essence of a Corporate Identity: the Logo

The most visible and commonly used form of visual communication between a company and its customers is the logo. It identifies and distinguishes one company from another, and tells a story about the history, quality, and type of products or services offered. Because all of these attributes must be communicated in a single mark, the designer is faced with a difficult challenge. In addition to what it must convey, it must also be easily and immediately deciphered at all sizes, whether reduced in size to fit a business card, shown for a brief second on television, or emblazoned larger-than-life on a billboard. Logos are the ultimate form of visual shorthand and the first step in creating any identity campaign.

There are two main types of logos: logo marks and logotypes. Logo marks are self-contained symbols of an organization that use unique shapes and graphics to convey the nature of a business. Sometimes marks use the initials of the company, such as for BP (British Petroleum) or ABC (American Broadcast Company), and sometimes they are pictorial and suggestive of the products a company produces, such as for Ossip Optometry. In either case, logo marks must be executed in a simple fashion to achieve maximum recognition and memorability.

The mark for Al Mal Investment is memorable in that it resembles the company initials as well as a person. Adding double meaning to a logo increases customer recall.
Design: Paragon Marketing Communications

- To tell the audience about a company or organization—who it is and what is does

- To be unique so it differentiates the company from competitors

- To be memorable, ensuring immediate recall and association with customer perceptions

- To be timeless in design to maintain longevity. This means bucking current trends that might date the mark.

- Most importantly, to be applied to all forms of visual communication in a consistent manner to convey solidarity and professionalism

This mark uses negative space and a bold, industrial typeface to effectively convey the company's core product—padlocks that provide security.
Design: Gary Davis Design

Ossip Optometry's simple mark uses repetition of the company's initials, "O O," to create a strong and memorable identity. The black-and-white mark's versatility will enable the logo to work in all types of applications.
Design: Lodge Design

This logo for the AllPro inspection agency visually communicates the company's mission; to inspect every nook and cranny of a house and leave no element unturned.
Design: Gary Davis Design

The Gamefrog logo is a striking graphic depiction of a frog with its head just above the water. The aggressively rendered frog is an appropriate image for a video game audience dedicated to fierce competition.
Design: Late Night Creative

The United States commissioned the design of a new corporate identity for the Department of the Interior and its various agencies. Each logo is distinct and works independently of the others while maintaining consistency within the group.
Design: Michael Schwab Studio

The Complete Graphic Designer

STACK THE DECK ™

By featuring a hand holding the "ace of spades" card, the nature of the company is immediately evident, making this a successful design solution.
Design: Indicia Design

Logos should be complex in meaning and concept yet simple in execution. This allows the viewer to easily recognize the mark, even from a great distance. Three characteristics of a successful logo and the order in which the viewer should decipher them are:

1. Color
2. Shape
3. Content
   (the organization's name and possibly a tagline)

Logotypes are usually less abstract than logo marks, and are composed of the letterforms that spell the company's name. Such is the case with the identities for Boeing, Charles Schwab, and Clearwire. Even though these are predominantly type treatments classified as logos, special care has been taken in selecting a typeface that evokes emotion and gives the logo a unique, immediately recognizable shape. Sometimes an embellishment to the dot of an "i" or changing the color of one word or letter can result in immediate recognition, such as with Clearwire's logo.

Logo shapes help customers quickly identify the company or organization they represent. For example, the distinctive bowtie shape of Chevrolet is instantly recognizable. BP Amoco's brightly colored sunburst can be seen on gas station signs from miles away. Even logos comprised of nothing more than a circle and an overlapping bar can be extremely effective and often imitated as is true of the London Underground mark. Simplicity in logo design makes for more immediate and memorable communication.

clearw i re

Clearwire is a broadband wireless provider. To help convey this idea, the body of the "i" has been made invisible except for the dot. Judicious use of color helps separate the two syllables of the company's name for more immediate recall.
Design:
Hornall Anderson Design Works

This logo for a coffee house in Kuwait loses some of its beauty and effectiveness when translated into English. When paired with Arabic, the outline of the cup beautifully coordinates with the Aramaic text.
Design: Paragon Marketing Communications

Al Diwan Al Malaki
Coffee

Association for Breastfeeding Advocacy
(Singapore)

A mother and child are rendered as abstract shapes in this logo for ABAS Singapore. A geometric typeface with similar circular forms was selected to compliment the design of the logo mark.
Design: Yellow Octopus

Plava Laguna, a hotel and resort in Croatia, literally means "blue lagoon." This beautifully rendered mark is suggestive of both sailing and luxury through the use of an elegant serif typeface and cool hues.
Design: Ideo

JINEN SABOH

For multinational marks, two languages must sometimes appear in order to be effective. Jinen Saboh is a Japanese restaurant whose logo incorporates both Japanese and English translations of its name.
Design: Tokyo NEWER

Choosing Color

Color plays an important role in the creation of logos and identity systems. Certain colors are appropriate for certain industries and companies; for example, bright colors might be more appropriate for new, technology-based companies, while more conservative, richer hues such as burgundy and forest green would work well for financial institutions. The most common colors used in all corporate identity programs are navy blue and gray, which represent strength and solidarity. Color is so important that companies try to claim and trademark the use of certain colors: Coca-Cola is associated with red, H&R Block uses green, and IBM is referred to as "Big Blue." When attributing color to a new corporate identity, it is important to examine all competing entities within the same industry and to try to select a color that will immediately differentiate the company. Additionally, assigning a color that may evoke certain emotions within the target market is an equally important consideration.

This logo for a bread company takes a very Modernist approach in differentiating itself from competitors. A highly stylized wheat stalk appears over a split field background that represents the land and sky.
Design: Paragon Marketing & Communication

The design of a logo may often incorporate the company name in some fashion. In this logo for a Web-based software company, "tri" represents the three different software programs that have been integrated into one easy-to-use interface. Three interlocking circuits dynamically and visually portray this idea.
Design: Jolly Design

126

The Complete Graphic Designer

CHASE

Changing Attitudes about Corporate Identity

What makes a logo and thus an identity system successful is an issue that has been debated since 1905 when
Peter Behrens created what is arguably the first extensive
corporate identity system for AEG (Allgemeine Elektricitats Gesellschaft, Germany). At that time, Behrens
did something unheard of in the design industry—he
applied the company's hexagonal logo to all facets of the
company's visual communication, including collateral,
products, and even factory architecture.

The first real explosion of corporate identity work began
in the 1950s and 60s. Saul Bass and Lester Beall, the pre-
vailing designers of the time, thought that logos should
be abstract representations of a company and that their
meaning would be derived from the perceptions of the
customer (one need only look to the Chase Manhattan
logo for an example of this type of thinking). Paul Rand,
then one of the preeminent corporate identity designers, insisted that logos should say something about the
nature of a company's business. This Modernist approach
to corporate identity lasted for nearly four decades, until
more and more businesses flooded the marketplace and
began competing for the same customers. It soon became necessary for companies to develop more visually
appealing logos that would grab attention and quickly
differentiate them from their competitors.

Corporate Identity

The Chase Manhattan logo was
developed in the 1960s and is an
arbitrary mark based on Modernist
design principles. The logo consists
of interlocking trapezoids and, as
a testament to the integrity of its
design, has remained relatively
unchanged, surviving multiple company mergers since its inception.
Design:
Chermayeff & Geismar Studio

The logo for the London Underground Rail system has been in
use since the late 1800s. Its simple
execution makes it immediately recognizable and memorable. Since its
introduction, the logo has reached
iconic status around the world.

The logotype for Amazon.com is whimsical and friendly and at the same time visually portrays that the company sells everything from A to Z.
Design: Turner Duckworth

amazon.com ®

portalplayer

PortalPlayer provides technology used in personal MP3 music players. In other words, it helps provide the music that puts smiles on people's faces.
Design: Cahan & Associates

Tivo's nontraditional identity was created in the late 1990s at the height of the Internet boom. A whimsical and friendly mark is used to represent the company's product, the first digital video recorder, and its relative ease of use. Tivo represents a thoughtful departure from more conservative media company marks.
Design: Michael Cronan Design

The identity for Breast Team is a whimsical logotype that is visually descriptive of what the company does, which is make breasts happy by keeping them healthy.
Design: Shinnoske, Inc.

This "new" approach to logo and identity design, where bold, flashy, layered graphics and colors dominate, was based on the design sensibilities of the MTV and Internet generations. It was thought that to make logos stand out from all of the other, more conservative marks already in use, these techniques would communicate the ideas of "new, different, better." Suddenly, orange, chartreuse, and other vibrant colors became acceptable to corporations. The typical sans serif type treatment used by so many huge corporations became taboo; personable and often whimsical type treatments were preferred to convey "fun," "friendliness," and to promote the idea that customers were more than just numbers. It didn't matter if the company was based on a harebrained idea or shoddy fundamentals; entrepreneurs and designers adopted an "if you build it, they will come" mentality toward corporate identity. At no other point in the history of identity design has this philosophy been more evident than during the 1990s at the height of the Internet dot-com boom.

As all things are cyclical, several years ago, in an attempt to speak to their audiences in a less-formal and friendlier manner, companies began to shift away from the extreme approach to corporate identity design taken during the late 1990s. Now, many corporations are trying to incorporate both the modern aesthetic and greater approachability by using conservative color schemes and "friendly" logotypes. Only time will tell how logo design will continue to evolve, but the debate will surely continue for generations.

INSPIRING LEADERSHIP

During the 1990s, logos that felt handcrafted or more illustrative became acceptable to corporations in an attempt to steer away from the cold and impersonal qualities associated with the more abstract logos that had been so prevalent.
Design: Greteman Group

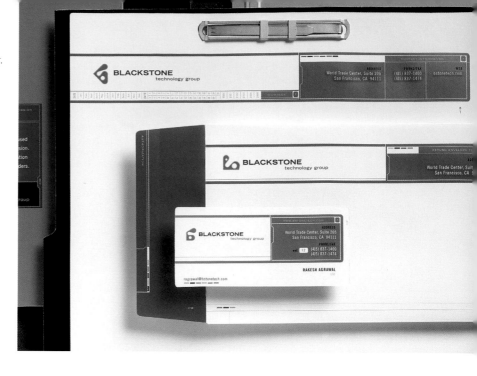

A very technical look was desired for Blackstone Technology Group's paper system, so a modular, grid- and graph-like structure was incorporated into the various elements of the system, including the firm's business cards.
Design: Templin Brink

Components of an Identity Program

Paper Systems

All of an organization's printed collateral for correspondence with employees and customers comprise the overall paper system, which is often referred to as the stationery system. At the bare minimum, this generally includes letterhead, secondary sheets (in case any correspondence is more than one page in length), business cards, and envelopes. In many cases, and depending upon the client's needs, mailing labels for packages, fax cover sheets, CD labels, note cards, and forms such as invoices are also required. When developing a paper system solution, the goal is to create a system that works on two levels—as individual pieces and as part of a cohesive whole.

Letterhead

The company's or organization's logo should be prominently featured along with the company's legal name (including any suffix such as Inc., Pty., Ltd., etc.), address, and phone number. Although many company stationery systems have the logo placed in the upper left corner of the paper, it does not necessarily have to live at the top of the page. In some cases, it might make sense for the logo to appear on the side or at the bottom of the letterhead, which is becoming more and more common. However, logo and contact information should not be placed too close to the edge of the sheet because they risk being trimmed off when printed. It is also advisable to allow as much space as possible for the content of a letter,

The profile of a woman is used as a striking graphic on this stationery for a fashion consultant. Deconstructing the logo and using the logotype and mark as separate elements allows for more design possibilities.
Design: Brainding

since most companies like to limit correspondence to one page.

Envelopes

Most envelopes for corporate identities use standard sizes, such as #10 (9 1/2" x 4 1/8") or A4 (210 x 297mm). However, some companies may have a need for, or simply choose to use, an alternative size. Regardless, the return address for the company or organization should appear on the face or the flap of the envelope. The envelope usually gets thrown away after a letter is opened, so including a phone number or website on the envelope is unnecessary. Keeping those specific details out of the public eye is best, especially given the increase in spam, telemarketers, and junk mail. Additionally, no artwork should appear on the bottom 5/8"(1.0 cm) of the envelope due to postal regulations in the United States.

For SOVArchitects, a clean system using black and red has been established to represent the company. Graphic elements reminiscent of light passing through an opening have been added to give the identity a more dynamic feel. This paper system also utilizes a policy-style envelope in which the opening is on the end of the envelope as opposed to the top.
Design: Hornall Anderson Design Works

Bahar & Bahar's paper system utilizes two spot colors and a clean and straightforward layout. The company name has been reduced to a simplified graphic mark, "2B," which is applied consistently across the various elements of the system. **Design: Paragon Marketing Communications**

Stationery System Usage

Each piece of corporate stationery fulfills a different need and, therefore, should contain varying types of information about the company or organization. Below are examples of the most common components used by companies and organizations, but depending on the unique needs of the client, the designer may be commissioned to develop additional pieces of collateral.

Letterhead

The logo, complete legal name of the company, address, phone number, fax number, and website URL should all be included on stationery. These elements comprise what is typically referred to as contact information.

Envelopes

The organization's or company's return address must appear on the envelope, either on the face or the flap. According to U.S. Post Office regulations, the return address must appear above the area designated for addressee information. For regulations and requirements outside of the United States, contact the design guidelines department of your local post office.

Business Cards

The same information that appears on letterhead should appear on business cards as well as the person's full name, title or position, and personal contact information (telephone and email address). Some people also include their cell phone numbers.

Note Cards

The company logo and address usually appear on the front or back of these folded, personalized cards. The inside is left blank for handwritten notes.

Letterhead doesn't always have to be white, even if it is printed on white paper. Because most inks are translucent, white paper stock allows printed colors to be richer and more vibrant. In the case of this paper system, the tan background of the paper is printed onto the sheet. This allows white to be used as a design element or to make certain elements pop off the page, such as the rule dividing the sheet or the white detail within the logo.
Design: Dotzero Design

Corporate Identity

By printing the letterhead and business cards on a soft, cream-colored paper stock and using chocolate-brown ink, this paper system for Witherspoon Woodworks portrays the quality and simple elegance of the company.
Design: Late Night Creative

The Complete Graphic Designer

Unique materials, paper, and printing processes have been chosen to effectively grab the audience's attention. The idea of layering has been used on business cards and letterhead to promote client interaction with the pieces.
Design: Bradley and Montgomery

Business Cards

Because business cards are often one of the first printed items a potential client or customer comes in contact with, companies tend to allocate more resources to creating impressive business cards than they will to other items in the stationery system. Unique folds, or die cuts, specialty inks such as metallics or varnishes, or even unusual paper are extras that can make a business card stand out and be memorable. As the old adage goes, "You never get a second chance to make a first impression." In addition to intriguing visual elements, the designer should communicate pertinent information about the person in a logical sequence by creating a visual hierarchy where the most important items are communicated first.

Note Cards

When a more personalized letter is desired, employees will often use note cards for handwritten notes or thank-you letters to clients or customers. Note cards are usually 5"x7" (12.7 x 17.8 cm) folded stationery printed on heavier paper such as an 80# or 100# cover stock with matching envelopes. Generally, note cards are blank except for the company's logo and

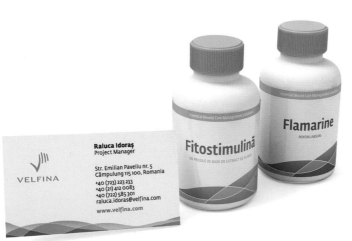

Velfina is a wound care management company. Its identity is very clean and professional, with a generous amount of white space and a minimal use of graphics.
Design: Grapefruit

Business cards make statements about the individuals who carry them, such as this card for Rofilco. Bold colors and simple graphics set the tone, and several cards use a larger version of the logo to create visual interest.
Design: Grapefruit

address, although an employee's name may sometimes be included.

Fax Cover Sheets

An often-overlooked yet integral part of an identity system is the facsimile (fax) cover sheet. This sheet will have the company's logo and contact information as well as space for the recipient's name, fax number, number of pages being transmitted, and a short message. Because of the method in which this piece of collateral is being communicated, its design should be minimal, utilizing pure black-and-white artwork. Text that is a tinted or light color, or grayscale images such as photos, will not only slow down the transmission speed of the fax but may not reproduce well when received.

Pocket Folder or Press Kit

The pocket folder is usually a 9" x 12" (22.9 x 30.5 cm) or slightly smaller folder that has inside pockets to contain all of a company's collateral, including slits for the insertion of a business card, informational CD, or brochure when appropriate. Because these are expensive to produce and are sent out less often, shelf life is an important factor to keep in mind. The folder should

The designers have taken a unique approach with this business card for a private investigation service. By silk-screening the information on plastic cards with magnifying properties, they have communicated the idea of "looking closely" in an engaging and memorable way.
Design: Kinetic

Rearden Commerce's identity consists of an "R" that is missing one leg. The mark, which resembles both an "R" and "C," is consistently placed on the left side of each piece of collateral. For the company's unique pocket folder, the logo has been turned into a repeating pattern that is printed in gloss on a matte sheet. The resulting tone-on-tone effect is subtle yet elegant and intriguingly tactile.
Design: Templin Brink

feature minimal contact information such as a website address or toll-free number that will not change. If the company relocates, this will prevent the company from having to reprint these costly items.

Another consideration is that the folders may need to serve a number of purposes, such as a container for press releases or leave-behind information. A generic design that features elements of the identity allows for maximum adaptability. It is best to avoid incorporating the graphics used in a current marketing campaign or advertising message, because these tend to date the piece and will ultimately limit its shelf life.

Most printers have standard "dies" or templates for pocket folders—there are many options to choose from, including one, two, and even side-loading pocket folders. Prior to developing a design, ask the printer to provide an electronic version of the template. If a client has a bigger budget, or a specific solution is necessary, it is possible to do almost anything. There are many ways to customize folders, including the shape of the pockets, types of closures, embossed graphics or words, die cuts, or unique printing techniques. The only limit to creativity is the designer's imagination.

EOS is a luxury airline that flies business customers between New York and England. The clean and modern serif typeface used in the identity for EOS reflects the elegance, class, and taste of the airline's target audience—the corporate executive.
Design:
Hornall Anderson Design Works

Vehicle Graphics

Incorporating vehicle graphics into a corporate identity program presents a unique set of challenges to the graphic designer. Any company that is in the transportation industry or that moves people or goods from place to place needs to have easily recognizable and identifiable markings. Delivery vehicles, such as cars, trucks, and even airplanes, are all extensions of a corporate identity that announce a company's presence. Due to varying sizes and types of vehicles, graphics may be produced in a number of ways: they may be painted, applied as vinyl stickers or magnets, or "wrapped" in giant skins of printed graphics.

Painted Graphics

Without specialized paint schemes that reinforce the corporate identities, all airplanes would look alike and be nearly impossible to identify with the naked eye. This is often an expensive part of an airline's identity campaign, because there are huge amounts of material and labor involved and paint has a tendency to fade over time. After changing the color scheme of their cargo jets from navy blue to mostly white, FedEx saved millions of dollars in painting costs.

A fold-over graphic standards brochure is used to communicate proper applications for placing the EuroEd identity onto all its vehicles.
Design: Grapefruit

HAWAIIAN

Hawaiian Airlines flies routes between the Hawaiian Islands and the United States as well as to several other destinations in the South Pacific, which most would consider to be a tropical paradise. That theme is conveyed through an elegant graphic of a Hawaiian beauty with a hibiscus in her hair painted onto the tail fin of the airlines' fleet of jets.
Design: Addison

In the case of the West Side Organics identity, more emphasis is placed on vehicle graphics since that is the primary method of communication with potential customers—deliveries "from the farm to your door." Because of this, wrap graphics are the best marketing option.
Design: Grapefruit

Vinyl Graphics

The least expensive option for producing corporate identity vehicle graphics is vinyl graphics, which are cut from large sheets of self-adhesive color vinyl and then applied to the vehicle. No gradients or tints of colors may be used because vinyl is only available in a limited number of solid colors. Systems that use special Pantone® or metallic colors may not be available so it is essential to inquire about their capabilities.

Vehicle Wraps

These large-format, full-color prints are applied to vehicles much like a giant exterior skin that covers all panels of the vehicle. These graphics are usually produced and sold by linear measurement and, depending on the size of the vehicle, can be quite costly.

Graphic Standards Manual

Successful identity programs must have reproducible, predictable results, regardless of which advertising agency, design studio, or public relations consultancy is producing materials. In large companies or organizations, there are often multiple people and departments that need to use the logo for various marketing purposes, but it is inefficient and costly to have an outside designer produce every memo or presentation that executives need on a day-to-day basis. One way to

Pokechu! Train's new corporate identity utilizes a basic color scheme (red and black) and bold typography. The letterforms of the train's name are used throughout the cabs on signage, banners, and even as a background pattern. Consistency is an essential element of successful corporate identity work.
Design: Shinnoske, Inc.

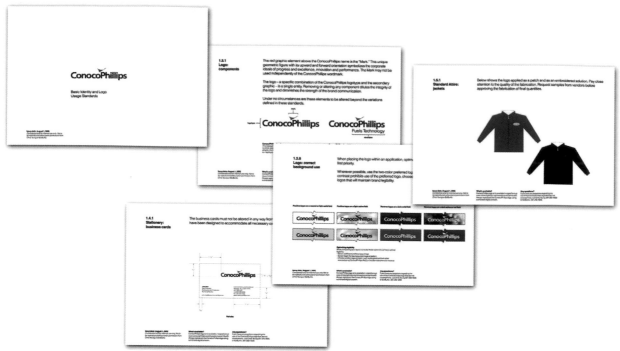

The Complete Graphic Designer

When Conoco and Phillips merged to form the third-largest integrated energy company in the world, the new identity had to be applied across various formats and media. The graphic standards developed for the company included creating the paper system, employee uniforms and hard hats, as well as guidelines for using the identity in advertising.
Design: Addison

ensure a campaign remains consistent, even with multiple designers, is to create a graphic standards manual. This document is designed to show all acceptable uses for a company's logo and identity in every possible situation, as well as show some unacceptable examples. Graphic standards manuals contain a kit of parts for recreating the identity including all of the graphic elements that may be used to enhance it. The goal of this manual is to ensure proper implementation of the corporate identity.

Logo proportions, sizes, and spacing issues should all be stipulated in the standards manual. Additionally, the designated color palette, including sample swatches of colors and their respective Pantone® numbers, CMYK, and RGB values, must be outlined. Most identities will have two color palettes for use with the identity, a primary palette that will include the logo's "corporate" color scheme and a secondary palette that might include accent or complementary colors.

Approved typefaces that correspond with the logo and logotype should be indicated with the appropriate layouts for letters, press releases, and other common correspondence. A good idea is to show scale versions of every piece of a company's identity including the exact dimensions needed to recreate those pieces.

Some of the items found in a graphic standards guide are the following:

1. Logo construction

2. Color usage

3. Type usage

4. Detailed specifications for recreating components of the identity

5. Examples of common documents and forms

Most graphic standards guides that are shown in design annuals or publications are extensive, custom-built binders containing dozens, if not hundreds, of pages. Typically, these huge standards manuals are created for very large corporations that have offices throughout the world and several advertising and marketing agencies of record, as well as hundreds of vendors that produce items bearing the company's insignia. More than likely, smaller companies such as start-ups or medium-size companies will not need such an extensive manual because they may only have one or two firms creating their marketing collateral. Instead, a simple one-page flier used as a quick reference guide for employees and vendors will keep the campaign consistent. Every situation is unique, so take stock of the identity campaign and be sure to cover all the bases, no matter how limited or vast.

To ensure accurate color reproduction every time the Opus Capital paper system goes to print, the designer created these diagrams to specify exact spot colors. Regardless of which printer is used, adhering to these guidelines helps maintain color consistency for the identity.
Design: Michael Cronan Design

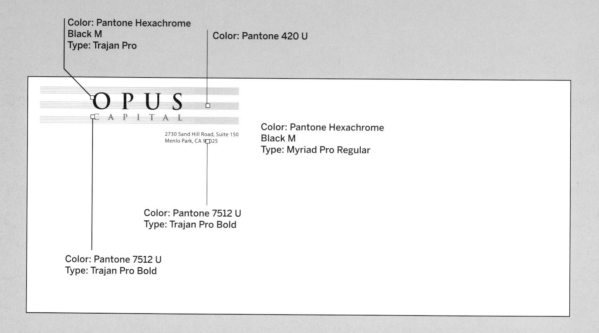

Color: Pantone Hexachrome Black M
Type: Trajan Pro

Color: Pantone 420 U

Color: Pantone Hexachrome Black M
Type: Myriad Pro Regular

Color: Pantone 7512 U
Type: Trajan Pro Bold

Color: Pantone 7512 U
Type: Trajan Pro Bold

2730 Sand Hill Road, Suite 150
Menlo Park, CA 94025

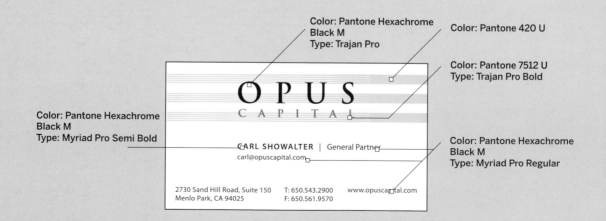

Color: Pantone Hexachrome Black M
Type: Trajan Pro

Color: Pantone 420 U

Color: Pantone 7512 U
Type: Trajan Pro Bold

Color: Pantone Hexachrome Black M
Type: Myriad Pro Semi Bold

Color: Pantone Hexachrome Black M
Type: Myriad Pro Regular

CARL SHOWALTER | General Partner
carl@opuscapital.com

2730 Sand Hill Road, Suite 150   T: 650.543.2900   www.opuscapital.com
Menlo Park, CA 94025   F: 650.561.9570

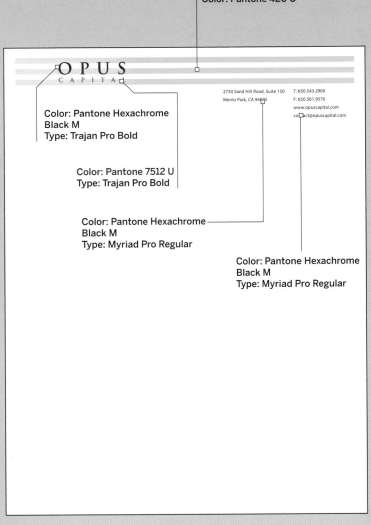

Color: Pantone 420 U

Color: Pantone Hexachrome Black M
Type: Trajan Pro Bold

Color: Pantone 7512 U
Type: Trajan Pro Bold

Color: Pantone Hexachrome Black M
Type: Myriad Pro Regular

Color: Pantone Hexachrome Black M
Type: Myriad Pro Regular

2730 Sand Hill Road, Suite 150
Menlo Park, CA 94025

T: 650.543.2900
F: 650.561.9570
www.opuscapital.com
contact@opuscapital.com

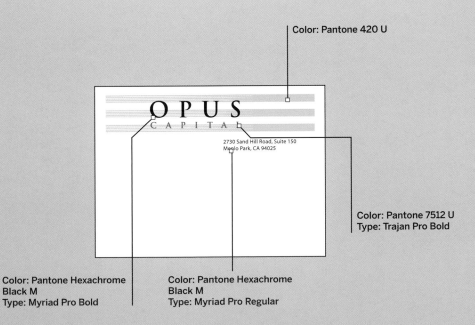

Color: Pantone 420 U

2730 Sand Hill Road, Suite 150
Menlo Park, CA 94025

Color: Pantone 7512 U
Type: Trajan Pro Bold

Color: Pantone Hexachrome Black M
Type: Myriad Pro Bold

Color: Pantone Hexachrome Black M
Type: Myriad Pro Regular

143

Corporate Identity

Shopping bags and gift wrap promote
retail brands such as these for Shin-
segae, a Korean department store.
Customers not only use them for
their shopping experience, they also
save them for future use, exposing
the brand to others.
Design:
Chermayeff & Geismar Studio

"Products are made in the factory,
brands are made in the mind."

—Walter Landor, founder, Landor Associates

Chapter 6:

Branding

Branding is about perception—the perception of a company, its products, or services. Connections and emotional appeal must be made between a company and its customers through the consistent use of graphics. For some, a brand is about social status, convincing customers that they can afford a certain lifestyle or that they can appreciate luxury. For others, brands are about attitude and individuality.

Sports team brands help identify players on the field of competition, but to be truly effective, they must be marketable as both memorabilia and merchandise. They evoke spirit and unity among the team, fans, and community.
Design:
Hornall Anderson Design Works

Brands have the power to make customers identify with a product or a service, to feel as though they belong to something important. They affect purchasing decisions, persuading a person to buy one product over another, often to spend more money in the process.

The sheer power of branding on an audience's psyche is a complex, creative challenge for the graphic designer, one that goes well beyond the traditional identity. Brands are much like corporate identity in that they require visual consistency. However, the application of a brand extends well beyond two-dimensional, printed collateral; it includes the entire customer experience, everything from the logo and packaging to customer service and the retail environment. The packaging communicates to the user how a product looks, what it feels like when he picks it up, and how well it works or tastes; all these elements work together to help the user form an opinion about the company, its product, or service. This is known as the "brand experience."

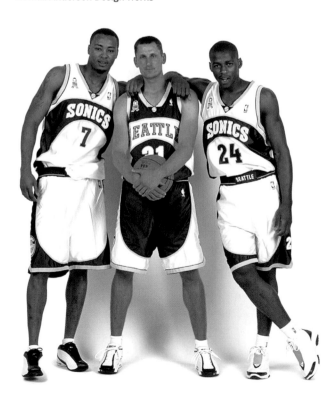

The Noodlin' brand extends to all facets of the restaurant from interior signage and store layout to packaging and stationery. Wavy lines in counter shapes, shelves, and even the "l"s within the brand's logo have been incorporated to convey the noodle theme.
Design: Sandstrom Design

The Importance of Branding

In today's ultra-competitive market, everything has a brand; even celebrities such as Paris Hilton or Lance Armstrong have a "brand." The reason for this is simple: branding sells. It creates a distinct image of a product or individual in the mind of consumers. For this reason, companies spend hundreds of millions of dollars each year on advertising and marketing to reinforce and evolve consumer brands so they remain "fresh." According to Thomas Hine, author of *The Total Package*, in an average half-hour trip to the supermarket, consumers are bombarded with the brands of up to 30,000 different products.

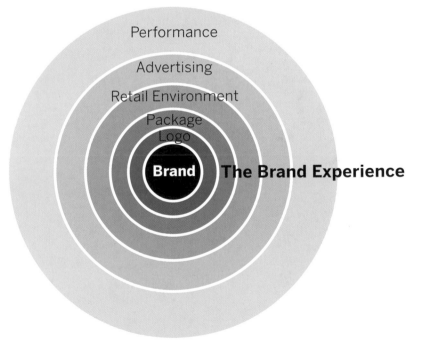

Performance

Advertising

Retail Environment

Package

Logo

Brand **The Brand Experience**

The brand experience starts with the core values and promises of the brand symbolized by a recognizable and unique mark. The brand package and retail environment help to sell the promise, while advertising is used to reinforce the message. Ultimately, however, it is the performance and use of the product, service, or organization, and whether it fulfills its promises that will determine its success.

To illustrate the effectiveness of successful branding, in 1984, Jay Doblin of the Doblin Group created a quiz called "Brand Frags" that asks participants to identify brands based on viewing only fragments of their logos. The brands represented here include Al Jezeera, Apple, Google, Nokia, Samsung, Mitsubishi, Ikea, and Starbucks.

The vibrant green colors used in this cosmetics brand logo and its distinct leaf shaped "N" are memorable and immediately recognizable.
Design: Ideo/Croatia

Branding Adds Value to Business

The difference between a U.S. $.49 cup of coffee purchased at a convenience store and one bought at a coffee shop for U.S. $3.00 is not necessarily the quality of the product, it is the customer's impression of the brand. In this regard, brands have the ability to significantly add real financial value to a company. Brands with positive appeal and vast exposure around the world are at the forefront of customer purchasing decisions, translating to higher sales and increased stock values. According to an InterBrand survey, some of the most valuable brands in the world are Apple, Google, Ikea, Starbucks, and Al Jezeera. Successful branding through design accomplishes the following goals:

1. It identifies and distinguishes the company or product from its competition, thereby building customer recognition.

2. It gives meaning to a company by incorporating all of the organization's core values and distilling them into a memorable form that resonates with the target audience.

3. It positions the company in the mind of consumers and makes a promise about performance, image, or value. Brands that are considered to be premium products or services demand higher prices.

4. It creates product loyalty through positive customer experiences. A happy customer will tell three of their friends about their experience and make repeat purchases, while an unhappy one will tell ten people about it and buy from a different vendor.

5. It communicates longevity and dependability. Companies that have tenure or have built a tradition for service instill more trust in the consumer.

One of the most valuable brands in the world is Coca-Cola. The distinct script logotype and bright-red color is unmistakably recognizable around the world.
Design: Cahan & Associates

Wildlife imagery and an earthy color palette of brown, orange, yellow, and green has been incorporated into the retail environment and graces posters and packaging.
Design:
Hornall Anderson Design Works

TERRAVIDA COFFEE

The Terravida logo incorporates a leaf shape as part of the "A," that when inverted becomes a "V" and a flame, to bolster the brand image of a natural product for active people. Complementary visuals are placed onto cups and product packaging for consistency in messaging.
Design:
Hornall Anderson Design Works

"Terravida" literally means "earth" and "life." To reinforce the message to patrons, the coffee brand uses images of nature juxtaposed with active people as part of its visual vocabulary.
Design:
Hornall Anderson Design Works

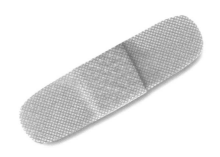

The brand names for these everyday products have become synonymous with the products themselves. People ask for a "Kleenex" to blow their nose or use "Band-Aids" to cover a blister or small wound.

Brands Become Ingrained in Culture

One of the ultimate expressions of a brand is when a company or product name becomes synonymous with all products or services in that category or when the name is used as a verb. People "Google" information on the Internet, "Fedex" packages, or make "Xerox" copies of important documents. Although there are many different brands of Internet search engines, overnight delivery services, and photocopiers, they are often referred to as these original brand names. Sometimes this is because the company or product was the first to market a particular product, and other times it is because the brand has saturated the marketplace and become "generic" to consumers.

Pottery Barn Kids, an extension of the Pottery Barn brand, uses a similar type treatment. Soothing pastel colors and fanciful illustrations suggestive of a child's nursery have been incorporated to appeal to this new market segment.
Design: Cahan & Associates

The "Mach 3" series of men's shaving razors is an example of a subsidiary manufactured and endorsed by Gillette. "Turbo," "G-Force," and "Extreme" are subsidiary brands identified by different packaging designs and colors.
Design: Wallace Church

The Complete Graphic Designer

Branding Basics

Types of Brands

Depending on the product, service, or target market, there are many ways to approach the process of branding. The brands of older, larger organizations already possess tradition and heritage, while young companies or start-ups usually require brands flexible enough to be adapted for product or service extensions. Taking into account the history, needs, and target audience of the client will enable the designer to determine what type of brand he is working with and thus what strategy will be most effective:

Arcelik is a Turkish company that manufactures and sells home appliances in Europe and Russia. Its monolithic identity is applied to all of its products, retail stores, and collateral because its established reputation in the market promotes recognition and credibility.
Design:
Chermayeff & Geismar Studio

Various models of automobiles use subsidiary brands to differentiate and develop equity in both names.

Seaboard, a pluralistic brand, is a multinational agribusiness and ocean transportation company. Seaboard Foods is one of the largest pork producers in the United States and encompasses two consumer brands, Prairie Fresh and Daily's.
Courtesy of Seaboard Foods, Inc.

1. Monolithic Brands

Brands with a dominant, established presence in the marketplace and within the minds of consumers are known as monolithic brands. Products and services are marketed under this brand name due to its recognition value and customer loyalty. The brand name is used in conjunction with a descriptive product name, such as Kraft® Macaroni and Cheese or Campbell's® Chicken Noodle Soup.

2. Subsidiary Brands

Subsidiary brands are those in which there is a parent organization with a branded subsidiary or division. Each brand is equally important to the consumer and must work in tandem to build a positive brand experience. Automobiles typically designate their products with sub brands; for example, BMW uses number designations for their automobiles, such as the "3-series" or "5-series."

3. Endorsed Brands

Endorsed brands are products or divisions that have their own powerful presence in the marketplace yet still benefit from being associated with their parent organization or brand. The Macintosh computer and iPod each have their own market share in the computer and consumer electronics categories but are still referred to as Apple products.

4. Pluralistic Brands

Pluralistic brands are large corporations like Procter & Gamble, Tyco International, and Mitsubishi that are conglomerate holding companies for many established consumer brands. When this occurs, often as the result of a merger or acquisition, a brand becomes pluralistic. The parent company's brand is transparent to the end user and unknown to most people except investors.

The Fossil brand takes a unique approach to branding in that its actual logo is not applied to any of its products' packaging. Instead, the Fossil brand achieves consistency and recognition through inconsistency, relying on nostalgic imagery and illustration to appeal to its core audience.
Design: Fossil Design Team

Most house paints are sold un-mixed and buyers choose a white or neutral shade that the store then custom mixes to the chosen color. Mary Carol Artisan Paints are sold premixed with the specific colors prominently featured on the outside of each can. The elegant and somewhat sparse design is reminiscent of fine art paints and thus communicates sophistication and quality.
Design: Willoughby Design

Brands Exist within Defined Product Categories

Products are organized into market segments called categories. Automobiles, wireless communication, computers, and shampoo are all considered different types of product categories in which brands compete against one another. But brands must also compete with other products on store shelves, each vying for customer attention and mindshare. It is the designer's responsibility to provide the visual distinction required to sell a brand, an increasingly challenging task.

The Drop Top image of a man and his dog in an open-air automobile playfully communicates the spirit of the brand. A limited use of color and distressed graphics in this microbrewery beer six-pack speaks to the target audience and effectively conveys the modest size of the business.
**Design:
Hornall Anderson Design Works**

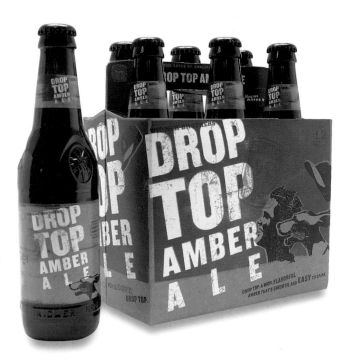

Consumers gravitate toward products with simple graphics. Upon closer examination, the viewer finds that these wine bottles appear to be zipped, playing off of the brand name, Bootleg. Novelty design ideas like this often entice new customers.
Design: Turner Duckworth

Defining the Brand's Audience

To develop and design a successful brand, the graphic designer must thoroughly research every aspect of the product, service, or company. Unlike corporate identity work in which design is primarily dictated by input from upper management, employees, and representatives, branding must involve feedback from the target market or audience. Some companies think they understand their market—which messages are most relevant, and which type of graphics are most appealing—but may have no empirical data to support those assumptions. Proper market research will determine customers' true opinions and impressions of a brand and what preferences ultimately entice them to buy a product or service.

Market Research

Market research is a valuable task that gathers and evaluates market conditions and preferences. Thorough and complete market research, which can include face-to-face interviews, surveys about the brand, focus groups, or mystery shoppers, can be an expensive and

The use of black and gold combined with sophisticated typography conveys luxury to consumers, allowing this jeweler to demand higher prices for products.
Design: Willoughby Design

The final brand for Sheridan's involved the input of customers and company executives in order to convey the messages of fun, hip, and cool.
Design: Willoughby Design

time-consuming endeavor, so generally only large ad agencies or creative firms have the resources to take on these complex tasks. To combat this, smaller design firms or freelance graphic designers will sometimes partner with a larger agency or hire an outside marketing firm to help conduct any necessary research. There are, however, many ways of conducting research that are less costly and can be done by even one person and many are outlined in the book, *A Graphic Designer's Research Guide*. Regardless of the client's or designer's resources, it is important to conduct as much research as possible; the results will always be well worth the time invested.

Types of Market Research:

1. Surveys and Interviews
Specific information about a potential customer's perceptions and opinions of a brand can be collected and analyzed through surveys and face-to-face interactions.

2. Focus Groups
Customers with similar attributes such as age, ethnicity, or income are paid a small fee to meet and discuss a particular product and its features, packaging, and advertising. Because these encounters are usually recorded on video, the people being interviewed may not respond as honestly as they would in an actual shopping experience, but still provide valuable information.

3. Mystery Shopping
The only way to gather true feedback regarding a customer's shopping habits and preferences is to observe them in an actual retail environment. Mystery shoppers are paid professionals who visit stores unannounced and observe the behavior of customers and employees.

4. Usability Testing
Product packaging and design are determined through usability testing. Usability testing involves the use of focus groups comprised of people from various demographics to use a product and then remark on a product's packaging or design, including its aesthetic and functional qualities. This is a good way to ensure that brands live up to their promises of ease of use, performance, and quality.

Jack in the Box fast-food restaurants use red to suggest flames and heat, orange to represent good food, and blue on their beverage containers to infer the sensations of cool and refreshing.
Design:
Hornall Anderson Design Works

For TicTac packaging used in South
America, a predominantly orange
container is used to denote orange
flavor, green for mint, and yellow
with green streaks for lemon-lime.
When used in conjunction with images suggestive of key ingredients,
flavor is quickly and effectively
communicated to consumers.
Design: UltraDesign

The soothing qualities of this high-end soap are conveyed through a soft, feminine illustration and rich colors. The layout instantly communicates with the viewer by featuring a simple, yet bold image with the product scent clearly labeled in the center.
Design: Wallace Church

In addition to differentiating competing brands, color is used to denote flavor within a product line. Common color and flavor associations are:

Red	cherry
Blue	blueberry or vanilla
Green	lime or mint
Yellow	lemon
Orange	citrus
Pink	strawberry or watermelon
Purple	grape
Brown	chocolate
Black	licorice

The Marketable Aspects of Color

Color is an important part of the branding process and has the power to evoke certain emotions or stimulate action. Worldwide, red and blue are the most preferred colors, which is why so many companies use them as part of their brand image. Orange is the most edible color, which also stimulates hunger, while red and yellow are colors that tend to agitate when viewed for long periods of time—it is no coincidence that fast-food restaurants use them as dominant colors to induce sales and then the quick consumption of food.

In every product category, there are color schemes that are more appropriate than others. Brands should attempt to "own" a color within a product category for easier recognition on the store shelf and to avoid any confusion with the competition. For example, within the American telecommunications segment, red is "owned" by Verizon, blue by AT&T, orange by Cingular, and yellow by Sprint.

The whimsical illustrations used on packaging for the Bunna brand suggests its dairy products come straight from the source, a cow. Color is used effectively to differentiate flavors within the product lines.
Design: Grapefruit

Brand Components

Creating a successful branding campaign is both a complex task and a big undertaking for any designer. Because brands must utilize consistent messaging throughout their campaign to build trust with the target audience, it is the designer's responsibility to thoroughly explore and consider every element of a brand and its application before implementing any design decisions. Before getting down to work, it is always best to make a list of all the components that need to be developed and a detailed strategy for each. This time invested early on will save the designer frustration and angst by helping to avoid redesigns down the line.

The Logo: an Entry Point of a Brand

The brand logo is the entry point for a customer's experience with a product or service. These marks quickly define and distinguish a product or a company: who or what it is, what it does, and its unique qualities. Depending on the audience's past brand experience, the logo connects with them on subconscious and emotional levels, evoking good or bad connotations. Repeated exposure to the logo builds recognition and memorability with the viewer.

Both Russell Athletic and Mueller's are memorable brand marks that customers identify with. Simplicity of execution allows for immediate recognition and recall of past brand experiences.
Design: Wallace Church

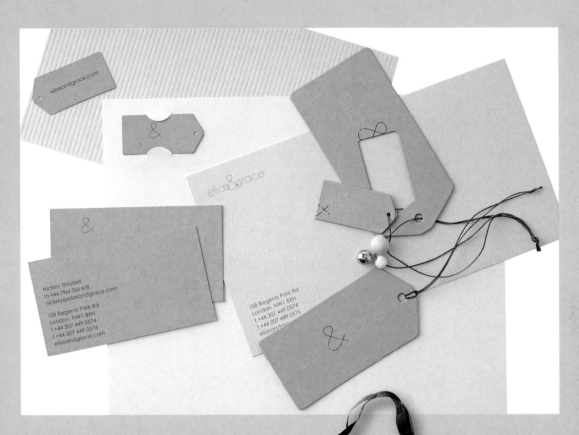

Elias & Grace is a modern, upscale maternity clothes store. Subtle typography and muted colors are used for the brand's identity, while the ampersand is suggestive of a mother carrying a child. Shopping bags are designed so that the ampersand also becomes a unifying element "tying" the whole piece together. Hangtags are punched so that they may also function as business cards for the store.
Design: Aloof Design

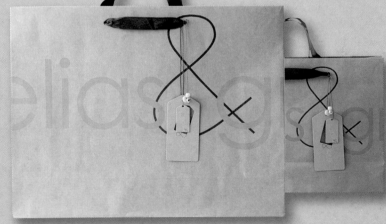

The halftone dot pattern radiating outward from the Zazz mark communicates to the viewer the carbonated qualities of the product and lends a modern sensibility to the packaging.
Design: Wallace Church

Minimal product packaging allows customers to interact with, examine, and hold this college application binder. A card-stock band introduces the product and explains its key features and benefits.
Design: Satellite Design

Package Design

Packaging is not only a container for the display, storage, or shipment of a product, it identifies, differentiates, and creates shelf appeal to entice the target audience. Effective packages showcase the unique aspects of a product or service—its benefits, quality (premium vs. economical), or physical characteristics (such as flavor or scent). As an important extension of a brand, its job is to convey the brand's messaging while positioning the product against its competitors.

Packaging Highlights Product Features

Package design should highlight the important features or unique benefits of a product. One way to emphasize key information is by using special materials such as foil stamps or metallic inks that catch a viewer's eye. Another way to inform and entice a customer is by offering them a closer look at the actual product through the use of acetate or cellophane windows. Showing an item can be an effective strategy because it reduces the mystery and buyers can feel more confident in their decision to purchase a product. For some items, the most important things are its features. By designing the package to include an extra flap listing benefits, features, or other pertinent information, a designer will promote viewer interaction; as we all know, getting the product into the hands of the customer is half the battle.

Striking product photography and minimal copy is both mouthwatering and highly effective at selling these pastries from Mr. Kipling.
Design: Turner Duckworth

Packaging Establishes Shelf Presence

A designer's job is to determine the most likely placement for a product within a retail store—and design-gripping graphics that draw attention to it. Companies and brand managers often offer incentives to retailers for prominent placement within a store or on store shelves. Placement of a product or package is an important consideration; for example, it might appear high up or down low on the shelf, making it easier or more difficult for customers to see when scanning products on a grocery store aisle. End caps, located at the end of store aisles, or special product bins attract attention and highlight particular products or brands, while areas near a cashier are notorious for containing impulse-purchase items such as gum, candy, or small, inexpensive items.

North Face's package system for tents and sleeping bags has an irregular-shaped container with a unique shelf presence. The hexagonal shape also allows for easy stacking of crates and boxes, and offers stores the ability to create dynamic displays.
Design: Satellite Design

Product containers come in a variety of shapes and sizes. A successful brand must use consistently applied graphics across all types of packaging regardless of their dimensions.
Design: Turner Duckworth

Offering products in a reusable container, such as the tins used to contain the Tea & Company's tea bags, not only increases the perceived value of the product, but offers the brand an extended opportunity to stay in the customer's view after the actual product has been used up.
Design: Cahan & Associates

Packages May Take Many Forms

The physical shape of packaging is often determined by the product itself, how it is used, and the way in which it will be transported from the factory to the consumer. Graphic designers must literally "think outside of the box" to create effective solutions that help propagate and enhance the brand experience. Many packages are ordinary boxes constructed of folded paper or card stock because they stack easily on store shelves or onto shipping pallets and are also more economical to produce. Although expensive, uniquely shaped containers and packages elevate the product's perceived quality in the mind of the consumer and increase its shelf appeal.

Depending on audience expectation, intricate or elaborate packaging may have the opposite effect. Instead of permeating the idea of quality, it may convey the idea that an item is overpriced, so it is essential to carefully research the target market to determine the most appropriate design solution. That being said, if a high-end look is what the package requires, an expensive or elaborate design is not the only way to achieve that. Visual concepts that have been thoughtfully conceived and well executed can be equally effective, it just takes a strong concept and a tight composition.

Clear plastic packaging showcases Charles Chocolates' gumdrops, while brown wrappers with playful swirls and line patterns are used for their chocolate products. The minimalist design lends an artisan feel to the products.
Design: Templin Brink

Unlike traditional beer packaging that uses amber- or green-colored bottles, Alcatraz Ale references the infamous penitentiary of the same name through the use of chrome bottles and "inmate" references on the cap.
Design: Turner Duckworth

Packaging Design Considerations

Many consumable goods fall under the jurisdiction of governmental agencies that regulate the buying, selling, and marketing of certain types of products. Sometimes these government entities require that certain information appear on the outside of a product package such as labels to warn about choking hazards or if an item of clothing is flammable. In many countries, packaging for perishable goods such as food must have product freshness seals, a list of ingredients, nutritional information, and package weight. In the case of medication, safety is a primary concern so products must be tamper-proof and have clearly labeled directions for use. Regardless of the type of package being designed, it is imperative that designers determine at the beginning of the process what, if any, essential information must be included on the final product package.

The UPC (Universal Product Code) symbol is a necessary part of any package design in the United States. Its placement should be easy for cashiers to find, either on the bottom or side of a package. For information on UPC placement on packages sold outside of the United States, designers should check their local government's packaging regulations.

3 00258 30837 9

U.S. federal law requires that all cigarette packages feature prominent warning labels about the risks of smoking. Several nations have implemented strong health warning label requirements, including Canada, Thailand, Australia, South Africa, Singapore, and Poland.

> **SURGEON GENERAL'S WARNING:**
> Smoking Causes Lung Cancer,
> Heart Disease, Emphysema, And
> May Complicate Pregnancy.

The Observatory CD package is unlike traditional CD packaging in that it is designed to resemble a worn diary about the band. Pages appear torn out, lyrics are scribbled in handwriting, and a pocket at the back of the book holds the actual music disc.

Design: Kinetic

Branding encompasses all aspects of a product, from packaging to supporting marketing collateral. U'Luvka Vodka uses a distinct background pattern that is printed tone-on-tone on boxes, cocktail booklets, the tissue paper bottles are wrapped in, and is even etched into the glass bottle. The entire brand experience is one of high end luxury and taste.

Design: Aloof Design

Papyrus is a store found in enclosed retail malls that specializes in distinctive stationery and paper products. Wood paneling used throughout the environment is reminiscent of a library and refers to the paper products themselves.
Design: Kiku Obata

Branding in the Retail Environment

Branding has evolved from focusing on the actual products or services to taking an important role in the entire consumer experience. Whereas fifty years ago most consumer products were marketed and sold through catalogs, door-to-door salespeople, or through other distribution channels, today most brands are sold in company-owned and operated retail environments. This allows companies to control every aspect of a customer's shopping experience from product placement on store shelves and lighting to having the ability to test products on shoppers. Even the way sales people are dressed and the manner in which they greet people are tightly controlled and an essential part of the branded retail environment.

There are many aspects to the retail environment that must be considered when designing a consumer experience. Every item in the store, from the window displays and signage to product labeling, must all be consistent in their mood, tone, and delivery of the brand promise, including the following:

Exterior signage that illuminates at night must be easy to read from afar. Backlit channel letters are used to cast a glow around the silhouetted letterforms.
Design: Gardner Design

1. Exterior Signage

Exterior signage appearing on the outside of a retail environment should be visible from several hundred feet away and, if open at night, lit up either through the use of channel letter lighting or illuminated light boxes. Stores that are free-standing structures may need to adhere to local building codes in terms of size restrictions and lighting regulations. If a retail location is in an enclosed mall or shopping center, signs will usually need to be smaller and have to adhere to the property specifications.

2. Interior Signage

Interior signage is used to guide the consumer through the store to find what they are looking for. Sometimes vinyl decals are placed onto windows to identify the store. Much like wayfinding, signs must be easy to read and comprehend. Where is the customer supposed to place an order, pick up an order, or ask for help?

Branding in the retail environment extends to the shopping centers and malls that stores occupy. To elevate the quality of a customer's experience while shopping, malls often create themes for various parts of the building such as indoor playgrounds and different wings. In each of these examples, lighting, graphics, and molded sculptures all work to create a branded retail experience.
Design: Kiku Obata

This clean, modern design for an apparel store is a good example of a branding campaign that has achieved a flexible system that is undeniably consistent. The window display, hangtags, and shopping bags are each striking designs on their own and convey the brand message in a simple and elegant manner.
Design: Gardner Design

3. P.O.P. displays

P.O.P. (point of purchase) displays call attention to specific products within a store. They are usually placed in high-traffic areas for maximum exposure. In a crowded retail environment in which all other prime shelf locations are spoken for, P.O.P. displays offer extraordinary visibility. Sometimes these are "bargain bins" for sale or clearance items. They may be constructed of laminated cardboard or other raw materials such as wood or metal.

4. Merchandise labels

Merchandise labels identify the product being sold and its attributes such as size, style, flavor, or scent. Usually implemented in the form of a hangtag or sticker placed onto products, labels contain a UPC bar code for scanning at the register and inventory control.

5. Marketing collateral

Marketing collateral is typically located throughout a retail store to promote the brand. Product brochures, advertising displays, credit card applications, postcards, and coupons are all part of a brand's identity and will reinforce a customer's experience.

This mobile P.O.P. for Castor & Pollux pet products incorporates bins for products, slatted sides for repositionable hanging products, and a display header that clearly identifies the brand.
Design: Sandstrom Design

The shape of product packaging for Castor & Pollux is unique to each product and its use. Shampoo is in a fire hydrant-shaped container, kitty litter in a plastic tub with an easy pour spout, and treats in a sealed box. The brand's lighthearted approach to product names and packaging creates a distinct brand image.
Design: Sandstrom Design

Developing a new brand for a national chain of convenience stores and gas stations encompasses many different elements. In addition to a new brand mark, exterior and interior signage had to be developed for all retail outlets. The brand has also been extended to fountain drink and coffee stations located within the store. Color schemes, typographical elements, and patterns all work together to create the brand experience.

Design: Gardner Design

The Complete Graphic Designer

La Cantera means "rock quarry" in Spanish, upon which this outdoor shopping center is built. Colored glass stones adorn signage at the retail location to reinforce the idea of precious stones. In celebration of the wild flowers that grow on the hillsides of Texas Hill Country, this brand identity includes colorful images of the types of insects that populate the region. Seed packets are given out to customers as a promotional tool to enhance the brand experience.
Design: fd2s

Conclusion

Graphic design is not art, nor is it strictly commercial art. While practicing designers would very much like the opportunity and complete creative freedom to create an artistic masterpiece that will garner them fame and fortune, the truth of the matter is that design is very much a business and occupation like any other. Designers must establish relationships with clients, collaborate with them to determine specific needs, and help solve a visual problem—how to connect with the target audience so they will be informed about the client, be persuaded to do something, or learn important information.

Given practical constraints such as budget and deadlines, visual solutions must follow the form of their intended function and the complete graphic designer must draw upon the skill sets of commercial artists such as illustrators, photographers, and designers. They must develop a process for approaching and solving visual problems to create highly effective and unique designs. Most importantly, the client should always be an integral part of the design process; he offers valuable insight into the company's goals and expectations of the industry, as well as the needs of the target audience—more so than the designer could ever hope to discover through market research or focus groups.

As evidenced by previous chapters, design is pervasive in all aspects of our lives. There are several disciplines within the industry that offer unique challenges and opportunities for growth. Most designers will find an area of graphic design that truly compels and inspires them, whether it is solving basic communication problems through semiotics, creating page layouts and design for publications or marketing collateral, or solving corporate identity and branding problems. The complete graphic designer is one who is well-rounded and experienced in all aspects of design.

Glossary

Accordion fold
A zigzag type of fold in a sheet of paper where two or more parallel folds open like an accordion permitting the paper to be extended to its full breadth with a single pull. Also called a fan fold.

AIGA
The American Institute of Graphic Arts is the professional association for design.

Bleed
A printed area that extends beyond the trimmed edge of a printed piece. Bleed areas generally range from 1/8" to 1/4" (3.175 to 6.35mm).

Blind emboss
A design element that is pressed into the paper in lieu of being printed in ink, giving it a "raised" impression.

Body copy
The main content or text used in any type of printed collateral such as a magazine, catalog, or brochure.

Bracketed exposure
Multiple exposures of a photograph that are taken using different aperture settings, shutter speeds, and lighting to determine the best version of an image for a particular purpose.

Brand
According to Jonas Bergvall, these are "the collected experiences of a company, product, or service," a customer has. The logo, packaging, retail environments, and marketing messages each contribute to the resulting impression a customer has about a product or company.

Brand equity
Qualities of a product, service, or brand experience that are familiar to the customer and that have been communicated consistently over time, adding "real" value to the brand.

Brand experience
The physical qualities of a product that help the consumer form an opinion about the brand, including packaging, tactile experience, and how well it works or tastes.

Call to action
The reason for a sales or marketing piece, this sentence, headline, or caption requests that the viewer of the piece do something, whether place a phone call or visit a website.

Closure
The manner in which a designed piece such as sales collateral, a brochure, or a pocket folder stays shut. This might include a clasp, a tuck tab, or string fastener.

CMYK
The four process colors that are used in printing to create the illusion of full color. Cyan, magenta, yellow, and a key color, black, are printed by overlapping dots to give the impression of thousands of different colors.

Coated paper
Paper with a smooth and sometimes glossy finish created by applying a clay coating to the surface. This prevents ink from sinking into paper and allows for more vivid color and different finishes such as matte, gloss, or silk.

Collateral
Any piece of printed marketing material that promotes a company or organization, its products, or services, including brochures, sales sheets, catalogs, pocket folders, etc.

Column
Blocks of type set at the same width.

Column inches
The measurement unit for newspaper advertising that is one column wide by one inch in length.

Combinatory play

According to Paul Rand, this is when the designer takes two ideas that are seemingly unrelated and then combines them into a new visual image or metaphor.

Corporate identity

The "persona" of a company or organization that is communicated through the consistent application of a logo, color palette, and overall design to all forms of visual communications directed at its target audience.

Counterform

In typography, this is the negative space within a letterform, such as the interior of a lowercase "e," "a," or "g."

Creative brief

A document developed in conjunction with the client to help guide the design process, which details specific information for use when solving a design problem, such as project goals and objectives, demographics of the target audience, a profile of the competition, and deliverable dates.

Crop

Trimming part of a photograph or illustration so that undesirable or unnecessary elements are eliminated.

Demographics

Statistical information such as age, gender, ethnicity, income level, and preferences that categorize people into distinct interest groups.

Depth of field

The area of an image that is in focus. A short depth of field is one in which objects in the foreground appear to be in sharper detail while those in the background are blurry.

Die

Sharp metal rules mounted on a board for making die cuts, or a solid metal block used for stamping foil or an impression on paper.

Die cut

A decorative or unusual cut made in paper with a metal die.

Dot gain

When halftone dots print larger on paper than they are on films or plates, they reduce detail and lower contrast. Uncoated papers tend to cause more dot gain than coated papers. Also called dot spread and press gain.

Emboss

A raised impression on the surface of paper produced by pressing it between two dies.

End caps

Shelves or bins at the end of an aisle in retail stores where products are placed for maximum visibility to consumers.

Endorsed brands

Brands associated with their parent organization or company even though their market presence is powerful on its own.

Fibonacci Sequence

A sequence of numbers in which each number is the sum of the preceding two, such as the following: 1, 1, 2, 3, 5, 8, 13, 21, 34...

Finish

Surface characteristics of paper. Examples of finishes include laid, linen, and vellum.

Focus group

A group of people with similar preferences and attributes that are selected to test a product or process and provide feedback. They are usually paid a small stipend for their time.

Foil stamp

A finishing technique in which metallic or colored foil is transferred onto a sheet of paper using heat and pressure.

Folio
The page number and other copy in the lower portion of a page, typically a title or issue date if it's a periodical.

Free association
A brainstorming technique in which any thought, word, or idea that comes to mind about a particular subject is written down for further exploration, such as colors, smells, visual metaphors, etc.

Golden Ratio
An aesthetically pleasing ratio used in Classical architecture and design, which is found throughout nature. The ratio of two sides is 1:1.618.

Graphic standards manual
A manual created by a designer to instruct a client on the appropriate and consistent use of the elements of their corporate identity. Guidelines are created so that anyone designing materials will know the "rules" of how the company's logos, colors, layouts, etc. should appear to maintain consistency across their program.

Grid
An invisible framework of guides that allows the designer to organize and arrange elements on a page.

Gutter
The white space between columns of type or between pages on a two-page spread.

Halftone pattern
Reproducing a continuous tone image by photographing it through a fine screen to convert the image into a series of dots.

Headline
A title for a piece of visual communication, usually less than one sentence in length, which briefly describes the subject matter to follow.

High-context society
Societies in which shared cultural experiences and education allow for more symbolism and meaning to be embedded into the design so a literal interpretation is not necessary. (See Low-context society)

Horizon line
In a publication such as a book or magazine, this is the place where the majority of text will align near the top of the page. It is in a consistent spot so that when a reader turns the page they know where to begin reading again.

House sheet
Paper that printers buy in bulk and keep in stock for print jobs. This is usually a medium-quality paper available in both coated and uncoated sheets.

Icon
In semiotics, this type of sign is a realistic representation of an object or thing. This may be a photograph or realistic illustration of the object being represented.

Idea tree
A brainstorming technique in which an idea or concept is written down and circled, and then related topics branch out from this core idea.

Index
In semiotics, this type of sign references an object or thing, but does not necessarily resemble the actual signified object (such as a biohazard sign).

Kerning
The spacing between individual letterforms.

Kinetic identity
A corporate identity in which various iterations of a logo mark or logo type may be used in different manners and not necessarily appear in a consistent place on printed collateral. Patterns, colors, and images may all be incorporated into a kinetic identity system.

Layers of depth
According to Marty Neuemeier, there are seven layers of depth in visual communication: perception, sensation, emotion, intellect, identification, reverberation, and spirituality.

Leading
The space between lines of text or copy.

Letterpress
A printing technique in which ink is pressed onto a sheet of paper via raised metal or wood.

Live area
The space between the page margins and gutter in which body copy or images can appear without the possibility of being trimmed off or obscured when printed.

Logomark
A self-contained symbol of a company or organization that uses unique shapes and graphics to convey the essence of a company.

Logotype
A typographic solution to a logo design problem that is made up of unique letterforms.

Low-context society
Societies in which information is transmitted via bullet point text and through the use of literal imagery and design rather than symbolism. (See High-context society)

Margins
The area around the outside of a page in which no text or images should be placed except for page numbers or elements that will bleed off the page.

Market research
The study of a company, organization, or product's target audience, including demographics, buying preferences, opinions, and perceptions of the brand.

Metallic varnish
A varnish mixed with a small amount of metallic ink. When viewed in the right light, a slight sheen is visible.

Mock ups
Prototypes of a design solution that are representative of how the final printed piece will be produced.

Modernism
One of the last great ideological movements in art and design in which clean shapes, structure, and layout were preferred and incorporated into design. Heavily inspired by the International Typographic Style ("Swiss design"), Modernism flourished from the 1940s through the 1960s and 1970s.

Module
Individual cells created by incorporating a grid structure into design and determined by columns and rows.

Monogram
A visual symbol of individuality composed of the first letters of a name.

Monolithic brands
Brands in which all products are marketed under a dominant brand name.

Negative space
Also known as "white space," these are open areas within a composition in which no text, images, or design elements are placed.

Offset lithography
Most common method of printing where an image on a plate is "offset" onto a rubber blanket cylinder that, in turn, transfers the image to a sheet of paper.

Orphan
When only one line of text appears at the top of a new column of text and is therefore separated from the rest of a paragraph of text.

Page trim

The physical dimensions of a printed piece. For example, a standard page size for correspondence in the United States is "trimmed," or cut, to 8.5" wide x 11" high (21.6 x 27.94 cm).

Pluralistic brands

When a company or organization has many different brands that it sells or markets under different brand names. Although all are related, this fact is transparent to the customer.

Points and picas

Units of measurements in page layout and design that are universally understood by printers around the world and should be used when specifying page or composition dimensions.

P.O.P.

Stands for "point of purchase," which is a display placed in high traffic areas of a retail environment to grab customers' attention.

Pantone/PMS

The Pantone® Matching System is the definitive international reference for selecting, specifying, matching, and controlling ink colors.

Paper system

Also called a "stationery system," this is a company or organization's letterhead, business cards, envelopes, thank-you note cards, facsimile cover sheets, etc.; as also, any printed piece of collateral that is used for company correspondence.

Policy style envelope

An envelope that opens on the short end of the envelope.

Press release

A public relations announcement issued to the news media and other targeted publications for the purpose of letting the public know about company developments.

Primary color palette

In corporate identity, these are the main colors used.

Printer spreads

Pages that are set up so they are positioned exactly where they will be when a publication is folded and printed.

Pro bono

A design project or job that is done for free.

Public domain

Images or text to which no person or other legal entity can establish or maintain proprietary interests; this includes items that are free of copyright restrictions, such as those from governmental institutions, as well as those in which copyright protection has expired.

Rag

A column of text contains unequal amounts of characters and words on each line although you should aim to have as consistent line lengths as possible. This uneven alignment of text is called the rag.

Reader spreads

Pages that are set up as they will be read (left- and right-hand pages side-by-side).

Recto

The right hand side of a spread is referred to as the recto page. (See verso)

RGB

Stands for red, green, and blue, the additive primary colors used to create a full range of color as projected light on a computer screen.

Rights-managed

Stock photography or illustration that is licensed, not sold, on a case-by-case basis. The designer may use a licensed image for a certain period of time, for a certain amount of printed collateral, and at a certain size. The stock photo house pays a royalty fee to the photographer or illustrator each time an image is used, but retains the unlimited right to reproduce and sell the image.

River

Large spaces between words in consecutive lines of copy that often occurs in blocks of justified text

Row

The vertically occurring spaces from the top to the bottom of a page or spread in a grid structure.

Saddle stitch

A method of binding by stitching through the centerfold of nested signatures.

Sans serif

Letterforms that do not have serifs or "feet."

Secondary color palette

In corporate identity, these are accent colors that may be used in conjunction with the primary corporate colors. Typically, they are used for backgrounds or other design elements.

Semiotics

The study of signs and symbols.

Serif

Letterforms that have serifs or "feet." They are generally easier to read when used with large amounts of copy.

Sign

Something that stands for something else. A sign is composed of a signified (the object or thing) and a signifier (what is used to represent that thing or object).

Signage

Graphics that help direct a viewer to a destination.

Silk screen

A method of printing where ink is forced through a stencil adhered to a screen. Also called serigraphy and screen printing.

Spread

Pages within a bound document that when opened are side by side.

Stock

Used in reference to illustration or photography that is readily available for purchase or licensing. These images are more "generic" looking and available for anyone to purchase.

Subsidiary brands

Brands where a parent organization has a branded subsidiary or division.

Symbol

In semiotics, this type of sign is an arbitrary signifier that has no apparent resemblance to an object or thing. It typically has a meaning that must be learned through culture or experience, such as a biohazard sign.

Target audience

The intended receiver of a visual message.

Thumbnail sketches

Quickly drawn sketches that communicate the designer's initial brainstorming of a visual solution. These allow for quick exploration of many variations of an idea in attempt to weed out the good ideas from the bad.

Tone-on-tone

An effect in which a design element appears to blend in with the background it is on. The use of blind embossing, spot varnishes, and other finishes are ways of creating this subtle effect.

Translucent
A substance or item such as paper that allows light to pass through it.

Uncoated paper
A paper that does not contain a special coating. Uncoated paper allows ink to be absorbed into the paper fibers resulting in colors that often appear muted.

Usability testing
A focus group comprised of people from various demographics that remark on a process or a product's packaging or design, including its aesthetic and functional qualities.

Varnishes
Clear inks that are available in dull or gloss finish. When used with full-color printing, they help "seal" the artwork.

Verso
The left page of a spread is the verso page. (See recto)

Vinyl graphics
Sheets of adhesive vinyl that are cut into shapes and letterforms and then applied to surfaces including windows, signs, and vehicles.

Violator
Starbursts or other graphic devices that are applied to a design to call attention to an important piece of information. They "violate" the integrity of the design and are best avoided.

Visual hierarchy
The organization and arrangement of design elements that help lead the viewer's eye throughout a composition. The purpose is to influence the order in which information is received.

Visual vocabulary
The type of images, graphics, and colors that a target audience prefers and is used to seeing. Examining competing companies, products, or services, as well as the hobbies or interests of the intended receiver determine what elements are most effective.

Wayfinding
Another term for directional signage that guides people from place to place.

Widow
When only one word appears on a line of text.

X-height
In typography, this is the height of lowercase letters within a type family. Traditionally, the larger or taller the x-height, the easier a font is to read.

Selected
Bibliography

Carter, Rob. **Typographic Design: Form and Communication.** New York: Van Nostrand Reinhold, 1993.

Crow, David. **Visible Signs.** Switzerland: AVA Publishing SA, 2003.

Gibson, Clare. **Signs & Symbols.** New York: Saraband Inc., 1996.

Johnson, Michael. **Problem Solved.** London: Phaidon Press Limited, 2002.

Lidwell, William et al. **Universal Principles of Design.** Massachusetts: Rockport Publishers, 2003.

Meggs, Philip B. **A History of Graphic Design**–2nd ed. New York: Van Nostrand Reinhold, 1992.

Mollerup, Per. **Marks of Excellence.** London: Phaidon Press Limited, 1997.

Neumeier, Marty. **The Brand Gap.** Berkeley: New Riders Publishing, 2003.

Newark, Quentin. **What is Graphic Design.** Switzerland: RotoVision SA, 2002.

Pipes, Alan. **Production for Graphic Designers.** New York: The Overlook Press, 2001.

Rand, Paul. **A Designer's Art.** New Haven: Yale University Press, 1985.

Wheeler, Alina. **Designing Brand Identity.** New Jersey: John Wiley & Sons, 2003.

Directory of
Contributors

Addison
20 Exchange Place
New York, NY 10005
USA
Phone: 212.229.5000
Fax: 212.929.3010

50 Osgood Place
San Francisco, CA 94133
USA
Phone: 415.956.7575
Fax: 415.433.8641
www.addison.com

Aloof Design
5 Fisher Street
Lewes
East Sussex
United Kingdom
BN7 2DG
Phone: +44 1273 470 887
www.aloofdesign.com

And Partners
156 Fifth Avenue, Suite 1234
New York, NY 10010
USA
Phone: 212.414.4700
Fax: 212.414.2915
www.andpartnersny.com

Archrival
720 O Street
Lincoln, NE 68508
USA
Phone: 402.435.2525
Fax: 402.435.8937
www.archrival.com

**B Communications
and Advertising**
Al-Thuraya Complex
Third Floor
Salem Al-Mubarak St.
Salmiya, Kuwait
Phone: (011)(965) 575.1383
Fax: (011) (965) 575.1387
www.bcomad.com

**Bradley and Montgomery
Advertising**
41 East 11th Street
New York, NY 10003
USA
Phone: 212.905.6025

342 East Saint Joseph Street
Indianapolis, IN 46202
USA
Phone: 317.423.1745
www.bamads.com

Brainding
Dorrego 1940 Floor 1 Of. P (1414CLO)
Buenos Aires, Argentina
Phone: (01154) 866.654.2361
www.brainding.com.ar

**Clark Bystrom
Bystrom Design**
4219 Triboro Trail
Austin, TX 78749
USA
Phone: 512.762.2705
Fax: 512.358.8805
www.bystromdesign.com

C&G Partners LLC
116 East 16th Street
10th Floor
New York, NY 10003
USA
Phone: 212.532.4460
Fax: 212.532.4465
www.cgpartnersllc.com

Cacao Design
Corso San Gottardo 18
20136 Milano
Italy
Phone: +39 02 89422896
Fax: +39 02 58106789
www.cacaodesign.it

Cahan and Associates
171 Second Street
Fifth Floor
San Francisco, CA 94105
USA
Phone: 415.621.0915
Fax: 415.621.7642
www.cahanassociates.com

CDT Design Limited
21 Brownlow Mews
London WC1N 2LG
United Kingdom
Phone: +44 (0)20 7242 0992
Fax: +44 (0)20 7242 1174
www.cdt-design.co.uk

Chermayeff & Geismar Studio, LLC
137 East 25th Street
New York, NY 10010
USA
Phone: 212.532.4595
Fax: 212.532.7711
www.cgstudionyc.com

Design Raymann BNO
Peter Van Anrooylaan 23
8952 CW Dieren
Postbus 236
6950 AE Dieren
Netherlands
Phone: (0313) 413192
Fax: (0313) 450463
www.raymann.nl

Dotzero Design
USA
Phone: 503.892.9262
www.dotzerodesign.com

Eason Associates Inc.
1220 19th Street, NW
Suite 401
Washington, DC 20036
USA
Phone: 202.223.9293
Fax: 202.223.6537
www.easonassociates.com

Fauxpas Grafik
Zweierstrasse 129
CH-8003 Zurich
Switzerland
Phone: +41 43 333 11 05
Fax: +41 43 333 11 75
www.fauxpas.ch

fd2s
500 Chicon
Austin, TX 78702
USA
Phone: 512.476.7733
Fax: 512.473.2202
www.fd2s.com

Carlos Fernandez
Fernandez Design
USA
Phone: 512.619.4020
Fax: 512.233.6006
www.fernandezdesign.com

Fossil
USA
Phone: 972.234.2525
www.fossil.com

Gardner Design
3204 E Douglas Avenue
Wichita, KS 67208
USA
Phone: 316.691.8808
www.gardnerdesign.com

Garmin International
USA
Phone: 913.397.8200
Fax: 913.397.8282
www.garmin.com

Gary Davis Design Office
809 San Antonio Road
Suite 2
Palo Alto, CA 94303
USA
Phone: 650.213.8349
Fax: 650.213.8389
www.gddo.com

Grapefruit
Str. Ipsilanti 45, Intrare
Splai
Iasi, 700029
Romania
Phone: (011) 40 (232) 233068
Fax: (011) 40 (232) 233066
www.grapefruit.ro

Greteman Group
1425 E. Douglas
Second Floor
Wichita, KS 67211
USA
Phone: 316.263.1004
Fax: 316.263.1060
www.gretemangroup.com

**Hornall Anderson
Design Works Inc.**
710 Second Avenue
Suite 1300
Seattle, WA 98104
USA
Phone: 206.467.5800
Fax: 206.467.6411
www.hadw.com

Ideo
Nova cesta 115
HR-10000 Zagreb
Croatia
Phone: 385 1 3014 302
Fax: 385 1 3095 136
www.ideo.hr

Indicia Design
1510 Prospect Ave.
Kansas City, MO 64127
USA
Phone: 816.471.6200
Fax: 816.471.6201
www.indiciadesign.com

Jolly Design
1701 Nueces Street
Austin, TX 78701
USA
Phone: 512.472.7007
Fax: 512. 472.6744
www.jollydesign.com

Jovan Rocanov
Diljska 7, Belgrade
Serbia and Montenegro
Phone: (011)381.63.88.20.964
www.rocanov.com

Kiku Obata & Company
616 Delmar Boulevard
Suite 200
St. Louis, MO 63112-1203
USA
Phone: 314.361.3110
Fax: 314. 361.4716
www.kikuobata.com

Kinetic Singapore
2 Leng Kee Road, #04-03A
Thye Hong Ctr, Singapore 159086
Phone: 6475 9377
Fax: 6472 5440
www.kinetic.com.sg

Late Night Creative
975 Walnut Street
Suite 100
Cary, NC 27511
USA
Phone: 919.465.2530
Fax: 919.465.4465

122 N. Avondale Road
Suite B-1
Avondale Estates, GA 30002
USA
Phone: 678.886.1994
www.latenightcreative.com

Lodge Design
7 South Johnson Avenue
Indianapolis. IN 46219
USA
Phone: 317.375.4399
Fax: 317.375.4398
www.lodgedesign.com

Manic Design
64 Jalan Kelabu Asap
Singapore 278257
Phone: (011) 65.6324-2008
Fax: (011) 65.6234-6530
www.manic.com.sg

**Michael Cronan
Cronan Design**
3090 Buena Vista Way
Berkeley, CA 94708-2020
USA
Phone: 415.720.3264
www.cronan.com

Michael Schwab Studio
108 Tamalpais Avenue
San Anselmo, CA 94960
USA
Phone: 415.257.5792
Fax: 415.257.5793
www.michaelschwab.com

Modern Dog
7903 Greenwood Ave. N
Seattle, WA 98103
USA
Phone: 206.789.7667
www.moderndog.com

Marty Neumeier
Neutron LLC
444 De Haro Street
Suite 212
San Francisco, CA 94107
USA
Phone: 415.626.9700
www.neutronllc.com

Paragon Marketing
Communications
Al-Fanar Mall, 1st Floor, Salem
Al Mubarak St., Off. 21J,
Salmiya
Kuwait
Phone: (011) 965.5716063/
068/ 039
Fax: (011) 965.5715985
www.paragonmc.com

Pentagram
11 Needham Road
London W11 2RP
United Kingdom
Phone: (011) 44 (0) 20 7229
3477
Fax: (011) 44 (0) 20 7727 9932

1508 West Fifth Street
Austin, Texas 78703
USA
Phone: 512.476.3076
Fax: 512.476.5725
www.pentagram.com

SamataMason
101 South First Street
West Dundee, IL 60118
USA
Phone: 847.428.8600
Fax: 847.428.6564

601–289 Alexander Street
Vancouver, BC V6A 4H6
Phone: 604.684.6060
Fax: 604.684.4274
www.samatamason.com

Sandstrom Design
808 SW Third Avenue
Suite 610
Portland, OR 97204
USA
Phone: 503.248.9466
Fax: 503.227.5035
www.sandstromdesign.com

Satellite Design
539 Bryant Street
Suite 305
San Francisco, CA 94107
USA
Phone: 415.371.1610
Fax: 415. 371.0458
www.satellite-design.com

Seaboard Foods
9000 W. 67th Street
Suite 200
Merriam, KS 66202
USA
Phone: 913.261.2100
www.seaboardfoods.com

Shinnoske Inc. Studio
2-1-8-602 Tsuriganecho
Chuoku Osaka 540-0035
Japan
Phone: (011) 81-6-6943-9077
Fax: (011) 81-6-6943-9078
www.shinn.co.jp

Shira Shechter Studio
19 Rothchild Ave.
Tel Aviv 66881
Israel
Phone: +972-3-5163629
Fax: +972-3-5160291
www.shira-s.com

Adam Larson
Shrine Design
Boston, MA
USA
www.shrine-design.com

Templin Brink Design
720 Tehama Street
San Francisco, CA 94103
USA
Phone: 415.255.9295
Fax: 415. 255.9296
www.templinbrinkdesign.com